D15673Z8

Maryland's Vanishing Lives

Maryland's Vanishing Lives

~ *John Sherwood*

Photographs by Edwin H. Remsberg

The Johns Hopkins University Press

Baltimore and London

The photographs in this book were made possible by a generous grant from the Maryland Humanities Council.

© 1994 The Johns Hopkins University Press
All rights reserved
Printed in the United States of America on acid-free paper

The Johns Hopkins University Press
2715 North Charles Street
Baltimore, Maryland 21218-4319
The Johns Hopkins Press Ltd., London

Library of Congress Cataloging-in-Publication Data
Sherwood, John, 1932–
    Maryland's vanishing lives / by John Sherwood.
        p.   cm.
    ISBN 0-8018-4702-8 (acid-free paper)
    1. Maryland — Social life and customs.   2. Maryland — Industries.   I. Title.
F186.2.S54   1994
975.2 — dc20   93-25163

A catalog record for this book is available from the British Library.

Contents

Foreword

Work plays a larger role in America's national identity than in that of many other countries, where wealth or birth may define a person's status. In America, achievement is valued at least as highly as other determinants of social station. Why is this? In *Maryland's Vanishing Lives*, John Sherwood and Edwin Remsberg give us images that may hold some answers, and I will try to put those images and answers in context.

These Marylanders' working lives may seem to be throwbacks to a pre-industrial era, when craftsmen and farmers enjoyed a slower style of work and life, but they are not. Most of the jobs Sherwood and Remsberg depict resulted directly from forces set in motion by the Industrial Revolution. From about 1760, industrialization created a large number of unskilled or at least semi-skilled occupations. Work in such jobs was easily learned, repetitive, and boring. In garment shops, for example, the various tasks of a skilled tailor were parceled out to machine operators, who cut material or sewed a seam or stitched a pocket or lapel. In cabinetmaking, specialized workers each made one part or executed one step in the final assembly, never learning the entire process from start to finish.

The English social critic John Ruskin described this work as "mindless," unworthy of the complex abilities of most humans. In the 1820s, he helped launch the English arts and crafts movement to bring back craftsmanship and the skills it entailed. Skilled work required the mental effort of problem solving and the physical skills of creative production. Craftsmen performed all the steps in production, not just one repeated operation. They dealt with customers and suppliers and constituted an important social stratum in pre-industrial communities. In short, they performed work that was both valuable and satisfying, while the majority of industrial "hands" did work that was dehumanizing and required little thought.

Thus, one effect of industrialization was the emergence, during the nineteenth century, of the quest for satisfying work. In places like the textile mills of New England, the farm machinery plants of the Midwest, and the garment shops of Baltimore, there emerged a hierarchy of skill that spurred competition for "good jobs": manager, engineer, machinist, mechanic. College and technical apprenticeships were the primary routes to such jobs. In Baltimore industries, Mergenthaler

Vocational ("Mervo") High School and Baltimore Polytechnic High School provided avenues of technical upward mobility; so did apprenticeships at the B & O Railroad, Bartlett and Hayward, and other machine-building companies. The city's large printing industry found printers at Mervo and graphic artists at the Maryland Institute of Art.

Industrialization also led to an expansion of what we now call the service sector. Industrial workers, having left the farm, needed provisioning. Gathered in cities, they swelled the clientele of taverns, dry-goods and grocery stores, and the like. Employment in the service sector offered an alternative to unskilled factory work that was attractive to many, and it often proved a route to self-employment.

Maryland's Vanishing Lives samples the rich variety of occupations that the Industrial Revolution created in Maryland, focusing on some of the niches people have created in their quest for satisfying work. All of these people have in common an emotional attachment to their work. Their jobs may not be glamorous, but they fill a personal psychological need as well as a social one—a need for variety, challenge, and achievement.

These people also share a fragile position on the cusp of technological and social change. That is what attracted Sherwood and Remsberg to them and what draws our attention as well. How long will their occupations be viable? In most cases, as with the Furst Printing Company, technology has already eliminated the niche they occupy. Desktop publishing and offset printing are more widespread, dependable, and cheaper than ever. What keeps the Fursts going is their editorial and graphic expertise. This same technology has created new jobs for people like the Fursts, whose special knowledge, coupled with a computer and modem, enables them to work at home for publishers around the country.

John Sherwood's text and Edwin Remsberg's photographs allow us to appreciate the emotional dimension of the jobs depicted here. Images like those of the Curtis brothers' sailmaking shop and Buckel's store capture a rich texture of orderly chaos and personal enterprise that is in marked contrast to most modern workplaces. The faces of these people reflect that sense of individual purpose and satisfaction that good work evokes. The photographs speak volumes.

The great value of this book is that it makes us pause to appreciate the tremendous variety of skilled but unacknowledged workers who contribute to our complex society.

Dennis Zembala
Director, Baltimore Museum of Industry

Preface

I have harbored a dream of writing a book like this since the 1960s, when I was a young reporter writing a column ("The Rambler") at the *Washington Star* newspaper. At first, those columns were based on serendipitous ramblings around the city, but they eventually led me into the Maryland and Virginia countryside and especially into Chesapeake Bay country.

About the same time, television correspondent Charles Kuralt was crafting his memorable "On the Road" people features for CBS News, only *his* territory was all of America. I avidly followed his work, and when he found a singing mailman in Kentucky, a canoe maker in Minnesota, or a blacksmith in Georgia, I was inspired to find someone equally interesting in Maryland or Virginia.

I developed a kind of knack for finding different people doing unusual, interesting things. Folks living old-fashioned ways of life especially appealed to me, particularly when those ways were being threatened by modern "improvements." These endangered human species provided good copy and pictures.

Times changed, however. Two of the several newspapers I wrote for ceased publication, and another appeared to be heading toward a state of collapse when I left newspapering in late 1990.

That year, wondering if my own way of life might be vanishing, I began investigating the vanishing ways of life of others as a possible theme for a book. The swiftness of societal changes caused by technological advances and other factors made me fear that we were losing much of our working past. I wondered if there were enough of these surviving ways to write about.

Maryland seemed a natural state to explore, because it lives up to its reputation as "America in Miniature." It has mountains, rivers and lakes, farms and villages, a big city and small towns, an Atlantic Ocean coastline, and the great Chesapeake Bay country that embraces the once isolated Eastern Shore. And history is at every turn.

After much research, making many contacts, pursuing ideas and suggestions, I set off on many exploratory trips. Eventually, I convinced others, such as Robert J. Brugger, an editor and author at the Johns Hopkins University Press in Baltimore, that I might be on to something.

Through an introduction by Brugger, I met Edwin Remsberg, the freelance photojournalist who was to set my people to music with his portrait compositions in black and white. Working at the time with the Baltimore Museum of Industry on a similar project, Remsberg agreed that discovering and documenting vanishing ways of life in Maryland was a worthwhile project and that a photo/essay book would be an ideal format. After looking at many pretty picture books with unsatisfying snippets of text, I concluded that if what people were doing was worth photographing, it should be worth writing about, too.

My quests uncovered working examples of old-fashioned ways of life, in old-fashioned settings, sometimes surrounded and under siege in modern settings. I was not interested in Colonial Williamsburg–style re-creations and restorations. I wanted stubborn survivors—living time capsules, anachronisms, twilight zones.

The search focused on individualists who had been carrying on the work of past generations and in the same general environment, especially those who represented the end of an era. I looked for meaningful dust and clutter and for aged equipment and methods sustained in an unchanged workplace that had not yet been altered by modernization. I was also interested in mild eccentrics whose ways of life were unusual, and craftspeople who didn't realize they were also artists.

I traveled the entire state—pushing my rusted-out, 1982 Datsun along roads that turned from asphalt to gravel to dirt to dead ends. Some promising places looked downright dangerous and were reached through overgrown paths in deep woods, leading to confrontations with junkyard dogs, ominous "NO TRESPASSING" signs, and locked doors. I banged on those doors, peered through murky windows, and left notes that were never answered.

The trail also included exploring rivers and creeks by small boat, because the perspective from waterways differs from that encountered on land. Many roads leading to the water are private, but waterways are open to all. Observing, close-up, the last of the Bay's skipjacks dredging for oysters under sail during the early winter of 1993, while sailing my own little boat in and around them, put more meaning into my own love of sailing.

Following more research and interviews, I began ruthlessly eliminating ideas and subjects (saving them for later), yet always seeming to come up with more irresistible possibilities. I turned over descriptive lists of these subjects to Remsberg for photographic documentation.

In September of 1991 things changed again. I started my first non-newspaper job in Washington and began to worry that the book itself might vanish. The job didn't work out, so I left and plunged full-time back into the book once more, happy to be writing about people again, and in my own style. The more people I met, the more other stories I heard about that seemed worth checking out.

I found those who were about to retire, but some vanished before I could carry out my "rescue." I interviewed one 92-year-old man just before he suffered a stroke, altering his keen memory. Baltimore's century-old Century Shoe Repair Shop was destroyed by fire in late 1992 the very week I had scheduled a second visit. I witnessed the demise of the world's largest pipe organ factory as it vanished on the auction block, piece by piece. An elderly Baltimore watchmaker said he was not interested in being part of anything that was vanishing, especially if it was him.

So it went: "Too late," I was told repeatedly. "Should have been here six months ago, a year ago." Even worse was when I arrived after designers had destroyed interiors and exteriors in those dreaded modernization projects that erase all charm, character, and personality to achieve a homogeneous look. Most disturbing of all was encountering old storefronts that had been covered up by plastic and aluminum siding.

What continues to haunt me is all those I have missed, who recently retired from their unique ways of life. There are, after all, the continuing obstacles of old age, infirmity, and death.

Often, the traits I found most admirable in these persons were their blunt honesty; their stubborn independence and resistance to change; a devotion to work, duty, family, and tradition; and a complete disregard of public opinion. I also regret being unable to spend more time with each one to create a more thorough portrait.

This small collection of Marylanders is a mere sampling of a localized slice of Americana, an attempt to save a few inspiring ways of life that are fast disappearing—and diminishing our own lives in the process. We have but scratched the surface in our modest attempt to give another generation something to ponder, appreciate and remember.

Individuals similar to those in this book can still be found out there, of course, by anyone taking the time to bypass the super-bypasses and meander through Smalltown America, following the winding roads in the back country or even patrolling some side streets of a troubled city. The only requirement for admission to observe these ways of life is a genuine interest in those ways.

Slow down and look around before it all goes away.

Acknowledgments

No project like this could possibly be carried out without those who, in ways both large and small, make contributions along the way. Edwin Remsberg and I each have a list of people and organizations to thank.

My thanks go to (alphabetically) John Barry, Steven L. Bunoski, Linda Cady, Estelle Carroll, Frank Dobson, Phil Evans, Vera Freeman, Winston Groom, Fred Hansen, Burt Hoffman, Tom Hoy, Joe Marzullo, Tom Nugent, Jane Sims Podesta, Ted Stanley, and Joe Wilkes.

Thanks also to my sons, Mark, Eric, and Scott, who shared a continuing interest in my findings; to my long-suffering wife, Betty; and my brother, Ron, a non-sailing sport fisherman, who figuratively tossed me a line in one of life's squalls so that my small, inferior blowboat could share the pier with his more powerful stinkpot. And a special thanks to that loyal 32-year-old sailboat, "Erewhon." Because of her shoal draft, she took me far up many rivers and creeks to observation points that could not have been reached by land.

I also want to acknowledge the cooperation of the American Association of Retired Persons, the Maryland Office of Tourism Development, the Department of Natural Resources, and other state agencies. Special thanks are due Bay writers Tom Horton, William Warner, and Robert Burgess; Bay photographers Marion Warren, Bob Grieser, David Harp, and Robert de Gast; *Sunpapers* reporters Jacques Kelly and Raphael Alvarez, and *Washington Post* reporter Eugene Meyer, all of whom have proven in print that they are as interested in this peculiar "vanishing" beat as I am; and to *Sunpapers* librarian Mary Schultz, who combed newspaper files for me and somehow remembered me as a young reporter there, and the Anne Arundel County Library system for locating books and reference material.

I must also single out just a few of many books that offered inspiration, information, consultation, and guidance: *Harvey Wang's New York*, by Harvey Wang; *On the Road with Charles Kuralt*, by Charles Kuralt; *Neighborhood: A State of Mind*, by Linda G. Rich, Joan Clark Netherwood, and Elinor B. Cahn; and *Maryland, A Middle Temperament, 1634–1980*, by Robert J. Brugger.

To those many other noble, worthwhile survivors of vanishing ways of life who were interviewed but not included in this book, I apologize. Maybe next time. . . . And, of course, to the subjects of this book, who endured my prying questions.

And how would I ever have done this without the patient encouragement of my editor Bob Brugger, of the Johns Hopkins University Press, who giggled and shook his head in bewilderment as we discussed some of these vanishing ways of life?

And, lastly, to all the others I'm thinking about as I run out of space in which to list them. But, of course, you all know who you are.

John Sherwood

Any project of this scale necessarily accumulates debts to more people than it is practical to thank. I apologize in advance to those whose support made this effort possible but whose names do not appear below.

I would like to thank the Baltimore Museum of Industry for the inspiration and support I've received over the duration of this work. Through the assistance of the Maryland Humanities Council, the museum's sponsorship of these photographs has made the images in this book possible. I am indebted to darkroom magician Trudy Slinger for her excellent prints and for helping to prove that there are photos somewhere in those negatives. I owe much to Dave Harp for his artistic and technical support, and to Jed Kirschbaum, Carl Bower, and Paul Souders. Their advice has improved the product before you. My thanks also to Virginia Remsberg for her support of the photographs, the book, and myself.

Finally, I wish to thank the subjects of these photographs for their goodwill and trust. Driving all over the state for the past two years and meeting these people has taught me that there is more humor and courage out there than I ever realized. I wish them all the best in whatever the future brings.

Edwin H. Remsberg

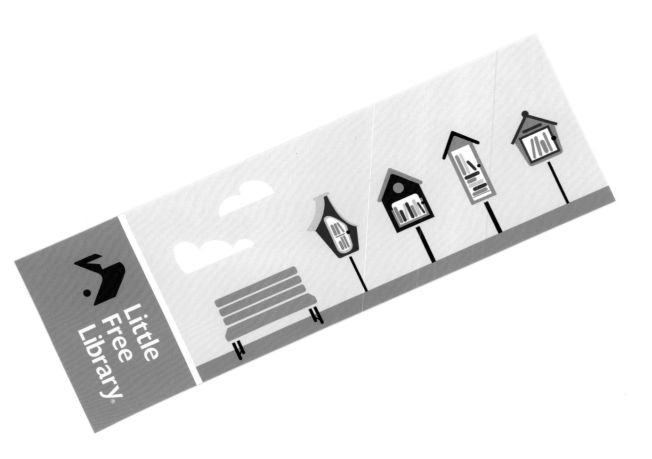

2

Sadowski Tugboat Towing Company, Fells Point ⁓

Much of the once-colorful dockside life along Baltimore's Inner Harbor has been edged out by what sentimentalists call the modern blight of urban renewal, which has relentlessly steamrollered the old ways. But a few independent mariners survive, hanging on grimly at water's edge because they know no other way of life.

Such a precarious survivor is the father-and-son Sadowski Tugboat Towing Company, at the foot of South Wolfe Street in once-gritty, now trendy Fells Point. The two operators, struggling with federal regulations in an uncertain economy, have a month-to-month lease but see nowhere else affordable to go. Jobs for these small independent towers have diminished, because many companies with barges now have their own tugs. Tugboat captain Jim Sadowski, 62, and first mate, son Marty, 38, spend much of their time waiting for a phone call to summon them immediately for a towing job anywhere at any hour for any length of time.

Working tugboats, of course, remain an old-fashioned presence, evoking memories of the way the harbor was, as they toot and tweet their whistled signals, although they rely more on two-way radios now. Outwardly, even modern tugs retain the old "Big Toot" profiles and still serve as the workhorses of the nation's waterways and harbors, moving ships and barges loaded with cargo, equipment, fuel, and supplies.

Many of today's modern tugs don't have wooden wheels in the wheelhouse. They use levers to steer. But the workhorse Sadowski tug still has a working wooden wheel, along with steering levers. The busiest of their three tugs is the 42-year-old "Gar-Den S.," a seventy-footer of 126 gross tons, generating 1,200 horsepower and carrying 8,000 gallons of diesel fuel.

Their pier bears a ponderous load of maritime paraphernalia accumulated over a fifty-year span dating from the founding of the firm by the late Jim Sadowski, Sr., near the end of World War II. They are penned in by encroaching condos, restaurants, and marinas, where once their neighbors were warehouses and smelly canneries.

"Business has been lousy and is getting worse all the time," says Captain Jim, a short, stocky man who began tending dock lines for his father at the age of 14. Marty, a gifted mechanic, dreams of one day converting the business to yacht maintenance, but his father is not comfortable working on boats that move underfoot when he steps aboard. It is unlikely that another generation of Sadowskis will run the firm. Marty says his oldest son, Greg, 10, is "going to college, although he loves to help work the tug with Pop and Pop-Pop. But mark my works, there will be a marina here, too, one day, and this operation will join the list of Inner Harbor memories."

When father and son are not maintaining their small fleet of three tugs, they can be found in their incredibly cluttered waterfront shack, where they often cook up a pot of stew while waiting for the phone to ring with a job. "We can't compete with the big tugboat companies, and when they finish their work there's not much left over for little guys like us," says Jim. "You might say we're dead in the water," adds Marty.

But when they do get a job, they spring into action in a hurry. Jim scampers up into the lofty wheelhouse and mans a huge, old-fashioned wooden wheel with eight spokes and hand spindles shaped like belaying pins. He'll give a "cast off" hand signal to Marty, handling the dock lines on the foredeck, and back out into the harbor, signaling with air horn warning blasts that they are under way.

It's a wonderful moment when this classic tug, encrusted in hard rubber fenders and riding low in the water, is active and working. She snorts and smokes into action, producing a symphonic medley of stress sounds as she grabs hold of something that only a tug can handle—such as a 170-foot-long barge holding 189,000 gallons of bunker oil to fuel a cargo ship waiting in the Baltimore anchorage. There are bass grunts and heaving groans, chugging pistons and churning backwater, a chorus of horns and tweeting whistles squeaking and squealing, synthetic lines straining at cleats and bitts while transferring energy into a slow and ponderous tugging motion.

"At one time, this was work that never seemed to stop," says Captain Jim. "Now, at least for small-time old-timers like me, I wait for work that never seems to start."

The Flyboys of Mexico Farms Airport, Cumberland ⌢

Only a handful of grass-strip airports are still open to the public in Maryland, and of these fast-disappearing mom-and-pop operations, one of the most endangered may be Mexico Farms Airport in Cumberland—the oldest unpaved public landing field in the state, maintained not as a business but out of a love of flying single-engine aircraft.

The flyboys of Mexico Farms hunker down in battered, corrugated tin hangars. Here, in their open clubhouses, they work on airplanes, talk about airplanes, and watch airplanes landing and taking off. "You can call us survivors, preserving a golden age of flight," says Greg Teeter, 41, of Flintstone, who owns a dozen airplanes, which make up a way of life for him. "I'm the teenager of the group. Most of the real teenagers are interested in cars, not planes."

Located near the Cumberland Municipal Airport in the Blue Valley flood plain, Mexico Farms was officially opened in 1923, although it was in use several years before that. The federal government maintained the field (the grass was mowed with a team of horses) for almost ten years and established there a radio shack staffed with a meteorologist to forward weather reports to Washington for the air mail service. The government scouted the Alleghenies for suitable pit-stop or emergency landing sites "because the practice of simply landing on any site that appeared suitable from the air had proved to be risky," wrote James H. and Martha R. Dolly in *The Journal of the Alleghenies*.

A plane's range in those early days of flight "was limited by its slow cruising speed and restricted fuel capacity . . . navigation in an open cockpit, especially over mountainous terrain, was difficult and often dangerous," the Dollys added. Today, a light plane flying in and out of Mexico Farms cannot even refuel because the owner of the field cannot get fuel delivered.

Donald Johnson, 62, and family members have long shared ownership of this 60-acre airport bordering the Potomac River, and they live adjacent to the landing field. The two unpaved runways, one of which is lighted, are 2,270 and 2,440 feet long. There is no radio room or control tower, but there are wind socks for the 60-some airplanes housed here.

"This is not a money-making proposition," says Johnson. "We only charge $10

a month to tie down a plane, and if our taxes go up any higher, well, I don't know what will happen. But I love airplanes and I love to hang out at the airport with the flyboys. I'm not a pilot, but I like to fly and I often get the chance when someone wants company."

The airport provides a social outlet for the local airplane "nuts" and about sixty members of the local chapter of the Experimental Aircraft Association, which maintains a clubhouse inside a hangar. There is usually a mid-summer airshow, featuring restored and vintage aircraft, and "fly-in breakfasts" are held once a month from April to early October. The evenings are usually quiet, but the airport is never deserted as long as Greg Teeter and his "airplane crazy" wife, Willy Braun, stable their thirteen planes here.

Teeter, a supervisor at a gas transmission compressor station, and his wife head immediately to the airport after work and spend their weekends there, flying around and working on their mostly operational fleet. They even have a little one-room apartment set up in a hangar for overnighting.

"We have problems deciding which ones to take up," he says. "We love them all, of course, but my favorite is the 1946 Taylorcraft I found in a chicken coop about twenty-five years ago. I flew it to California and back." One of Teeter's buddies is Harry "Peanut" White, 70, who has restored his Cessna-150 and has a student pilot's license. "We all fly together in one another's airplanes," says Peanut, who voluntarily mows the runways with the mower owned by the Experimental Aircraft Association.

Teeter remembers coming to Mexico Farms with his father as a youngster in the late 1950s. "That's when I got the bug," he says. "I started building and flying model airplanes and took my first flying lesson when I was 11. I got my pilot's license while still in high school and built my first plane in 1974."

A couple years ago Teeter was reintroduced to Willy Braun, his high school sweetheart, at a school reunion, and they were married in the summer of 1992. "I'd say that 90 percent of the wives of airplane nuts hate airplanes," he says, "so I made sure if I ever had a wife she would like them. She didn't at first, but now she's more of an airplane nut than I am!"

Wedding day for the Teeters was a special one for Mexico Farms Airport, too. The wedding party staged a "matrimonial fly-in," with Greg in a tuxedo flying in his plane with his best man at his side and Willy, in a full wedding gown, flying in her plane with her maid of honor. They were married in the middle of the landing field, a reception was held in their airplane hangar, and they flew off together on a happy air trails honeymoon flight.

That's the kind of airport Mexico Farms is.

"This IS a Printing Office"—*J. H. Furst Company, Baltimore*

An old printed sign, with the type set by hand in 120-pt. Century Bold, announces: "This IS a Printing Office. Crossroads of Civilization; Refuge of All the Arts Against the Ravages of Time; Armory of Fearless Truth Against Whispering Rumour." The sign, not at all a joke, hangs in the office of the J. H. Company, a venerable Baltimore printing firm with an international reputation for Old World quality since 1904. Furst became famous in the scholarly world by publishing a large number of demanding mathematical and scientific journals and other extremely complex works, in more than thirty ancient and modern languages.

Although it could still handle the exacting demands of university professors, 75 percent of Furst's business today is rather ordinary, mundane stuff: unromantic commercial jobs, genealogies, small literary magazines, and the like. Only one of the former jobs remains. Furst still sets type on an old linotype machine and uses a hand-fed flat-bed press to print small runs of a "speculative quarterly review of theology and philosophy." Paul F. Peters, 80, who has been with the company since 1929, has "locked up" pages of type in iron forms for this scholarly publication for the past fifty years.

Norman Weiner, 79, hand feeds the paper for the quarterly into a 38 × 50 Miehle Press, one of two Miehles that may look as if they belong in a museum but are still efficient and dependable. Furst has been printing the esoteric publication for nearly sixty years, to the satisfaction of the clients, who prefer Furst's exacting, precise methods that imprint the letters into the paper, making them easier to read.

What does it matter that no one at Furst and few outside of the quarterly's subscribers could fully comprehend articles entitled: "Rahner's Transcendental Deduction of the Vorgriff"? Furst's printers, typesetters, and proofreaders could never fathom any of the exotic material they read, but they could read it upside down and backward. They used to proof the copy of languages (some "lost") such as Runic, Nepalese, Sanskrit, Egyptian hieroglyphic, Siamese, Chinese, Arabic, Coptic, and three kinds of Syriac.

Such assignments no longer fall upon the heads of Charles Francis Furst, 70, the firm's president, and his son John, 26. They are calm, studious-looking printers who speak softly and carry an awesome family tradition and responsibility.

The Furst plant is modern, although housed in an old, rundown section of town on the fringe of Little Italy. The veteran printing machines no longer in regular use stand like iron dinosaurs near the modern Heidelberg offset presses that replaced them. "But we still use the old presses because they are more practical for certain jobs." says Francis Furst. "They are slower, but they run forever and require little maintenance, unlike the offsets, whose upkeep is outrageously expensive."

In a 1952 column, Baltimore *Sun* editor Price Day paid a fine tribute to the Fursts. They had, he wrote, "an expertness which—in the arrangement of title pages, in the sharpness and clarity and evenness of impression, in the balancing of text and margin, in the quality of paper and binding—goes beyond fine craftsmanship into artistry."

The family printing tradition dates to 1870 when John Henry Furst became an apprentice with the Baltimore publishing firm of John Murphy and Company. He was followed there in 1875 by his brother, Jacob Henry Furst. Frederick V. Furst came on board in 1883, at the age of 15, followed by his younger brother, Joseph A. Furst, in 1888.

The Great Baltimore Fire of 1904 wiped out the Murphy firm, but the owners thought so much of the Fursts that they turned over the name, good will and whatever was salvageable to them "with much pleasure," since the work required "special skill and aptitude for which we consider them particularly fitted." At the time, Murphy was already printing scholarly works for Johns Hopkins University, the Modern Language Association, the Journal of English and German Philology, and others.

Victor J. Furst, Sr., the father of Francis Furst, worked almost until his death in 1982, one day short of his ninetieth birthday. He was the one who, in 1907, began hand setting the type for a limited number of copies of what is now a valuable first edition—the autographed, autobiographical *Education of Henry Adams*, by the American philosopher and historian.

That was a piece of cake compared with John Collier Pope's highly complex *The Rhythms of Beowulf*, where musical notation is superimposed on a multiple-accent alphabet. "It took the author ten years to write and ten years to find someone who could print it," Victor Furst once observed.

It would have been a difficult business for printers whose only language was English. One scholar, for example, questioned why his manuscript was printed in the Jacobite script instead of the Nestorian script. Somehow they all worked it out to the author's satisfaction, although no one at Furst understood a word of anything in the book.

In a corner of an upstairs loft, one wooden case of movable type of characters remains. "I don't know why we're keeping it," says Furst. "It was last used forty years ago. I just can't bear to scrap it."

Lining a cinderblock wall near the old type chest are eight "barrister" bookcases filled with hundreds of extraordinary Furst volumes, many of them mammoth. Some examples:

> *Corinth: Results of Excavations Conducted by the American School of Classical Studies at Athens*, Vol. XI, *The Byzantine Pottery*, by Charles H. Morgan, Harvard University Press, 1942
>
> *A History of French Dramatic Literature in the Seventeenth Century*, Part II, *The Period of Corneille, 1635–1651*, by Henry Carrington Lancaster, Johns Hopkins University Press, 1932
>
> *Coptic Texts in the University of Michigan Collections*, 1942
>
> *Accounts rendered by Papal Collectors in England, 1317–1378*, American Philosophical Society, 1968 (600 pages of Latin)

More recent, less esoteric works include thin "vanity" books, such as *The Cattell Family of South Carolina*, by William Cattell Trimble (1988), and *The Smiling Distance*, a collection of poems by Juliana Brent Keyser (1992).

Most members of the Furst family have pursued other occupations. It should be noted, however, that one non-printer Furst, Gertrude, ran the firm's office from 1930 until shortly before her death in 1986.

"Our greatest enemy is death," Victor Furst, Sr., once observed. "The old printers die and no one wants to learn the job." He never did quite come to understand or appreciate the less artistic offset process which, in time, took so much work away from his firm, for they did not turn to offset until 1989.

In 1979, Victor Furst contracted to print a quarterly journal then being printed by an offset company. Fairly fuming, he said: "The footnotes are at the end of the magazine, not at the bottom of each page. Why bother to print such junk? It will be a great pleasure to take this over."

In a small office near a sliding warehouse door, two walls are lined with photographs of professors who were happy with their Furst publications, along with a gallery of distinguished Furst portraits, some of them quite faded. All of these people are dead.

"It's a very competitive field," says Charles Francis Furst, the current president, who returned to the family business after years of selling business machines.

"Many of the firms who did the kind of printing we can still do have gone out of business. Printers died off, and the craft of setting type is dying, too, a casualty of offset."

Frederick Furst once put it another way: "You've got to keep a balance in your work between art and business. Fifty percent of each is the ideal thing. Too much of one or too much of the other is bankruptcy."

Charles Francis Furst laughed when he heard that quotation. "They were very proud people," he observed. "They may have been more interested in the quality of their work and praise than money."

Maryland's Last One-Room Schoolhouse, Smith Island ⌒

Maryland is down to its last one-room public schoolhouse, far removed from bureaucratic bean counters and practically in hiding in the remote village of Tylerton, on Smith Island in the lower Chesapeake Bay. The school's enrollment of twelve students is projected to drop to three by 1995, because the birth rate in Tylerton is near zero, young couples having moved away to the mainland in search of jobs "off the water."

In 1980, Tylerton Elementary served a community of 157, now diminished to under 100 year-round, mostly elderly residents whose ways of life are threatened by "summer people," who have discovered the island and are purchasing family homesteads for use as getaway retreats. In 1993, there was but one birth in Tylerton, bringing the permanent population of those under the age of seven to four. There is one church, but all stores have disappeared, although two pick-up trucks and two cars are still in operation.

Along with the people, Smith Island (settled in 1657) is itself disappearing, being reclaimed by a rising sea level and the combined action of tides, currents, waves, and storms. Some island watermen add the harvesting of seafood to this list, thus questioning the very reason for living here.

A larger elementary school on the island is located in the main town of Ewell, less than ten minutes by boat from Tylerton. Where Tylerton has one certified teacher and a teacher's aide, Ewell Elementary has two teachers and three aides along with a library, media center, gymnasium, and twenty-four students in three classrooms from pre-school through seventh grade.

The earlier Tylerton schoolhouse was a picturesque white building, with a belltower, potbellied coal stove, and outhouse. But it was replaced twenty years ago by a contemporary, natural wood structure with a skylight and beamed cathedral ceiling. Fundamentally, it remains a one-roomer. On one side of the room a pre-schooler and a first grader are taught by teacher's aide "Miss Evelyn" Tyler, 51, who assists Mrs. April Riggin Tyler, 26, with her students. Mrs. Tyler, a certified teacher, instructs a third grader, five fourth graders, two fifth graders, and two sixth graders. When the sixth graders graduate, they go off on the schoolboat with

14

other Smith Island students on a daily, round-trip commute to Crisfield, 12 miles to the east on the mainland.

Baltimore *Sun* "On the Bay" reporter, Tom Horton, rented a house in Tylerton in 1987 for a year, with his wife and two young children, who enrolled in the one-room school. Recounting that pleasant experience, Horton wrote: "Some things about the little island school you could not put a price on. An image of taking Abby back to school after lunch one day sticks in my mind: We were walking hand in hand down the little lane that serves as Tylerton's main street, passing from bright autumn sunshine beneath the shade of the big old hackberry tree that has grown over the path for more than a century; overhead, geese were calling. . . . I recall something from a Thomas Hardy novel—a description of an English village so rural that a butterfly might have wandered down the main street without interruption. It was as if I had been able to transport my family back in time. The walk that day was all too short."

The days of Tylerton Elementary may also be all too short, although a spokesman for the Somerset County Board of Education says the school will "definitely be opened" for the 1993–94 school year. Beyond that, however, he would not go, explaining that a decision on the future of the last one-room public schoolhouse in Maryland will ultimately be left to the residents of Tylerton.

Vera, Empress of the White Sands, Lusby ~

Maryland has many unique restaurants that reflect the personalities, tastes, and idiosyncracies of their owners. But Vera's White Sands Marina and Restaurant in Lusby continues to survive in the boonies because of the owner's determination to keep it alive, even if it isn't all that profitable.

Far off the beaten track, Vera's is a real lulu of a restaurant lurking at the dead end of a twisting back road called White Sands, off Route 2 about ten miles north of Solomons, in Southern Maryland. Aloha, and welcome to a Polynesian fantasy in a South Seas setting, where frozen cocktails are served with swizzle sticks that pop open to form paper umbrellas. Unsuspecting boaters navigating historic St. Leonard Creek, off the Patuxent River, come upon a hillside of banana trees and feel as if they've slipped into some kind of Bermuda Triangle.

The restaurant's thatched roof has been replaced, but the interior still has a reed ceiling held up by bamboo poles and is crowded with ornate chairs and tables, marble statuary, carved Polynesian figures, ponderous antiques, Oriental umbrellas hanging from the ceiling, curiosities, bric-a-brac, peacock feathers—and cozy nooks for romantic dining.

Vera Freeman, who does not discuss her age ("What's the point?" she asks), lives next door to her restaurant and marina in "Vera's Villa," her own version of an all-white Taj Mahal with a swimming pool in the middle of her marble-floored living room.

Vera upstages everything when she materializes nightly, as if in a vision, through the front door of the White Sands shortly before sunset. She has a vast wardrobe that changes with her moods. Picture her wearing a pink, diaphanous floor-length sari from India; jewelry, gold, and pearls hang from her neck, fore-head, fingers, and wrists. Conjure up a platinum-haired version of Nora Desmond in the Hollywood classic *Sunset Boulevard*, sweeping into her fabricated world of glamour and onto the center stage of her restaurant, where she is the indisputable star.

Sometimes a huge brass gong is sounded upon her arrival. One of the bar-tenders, Buster or Carlos, wearing a Hawaiian shirt and leis, immediately pours a shallow glass of champagne as Vera glides inside and settles down on a vinyl, leopardskin barstool at the end of the bar, across from a grand piano. When the piano player strikes up a Vera favorite, the outdated "Sheik of Araby," it's as if someone has waved a wand and commanded the evening to begin.

As mildly egocentric as all this sounds, Vera herself is an astute, serious businesswoman, fully aware that people come to see her and her exotic restaurant as well as for the cuisine. "I love being surrounded by all these beautiful objects," she says, pointing out the objets d'art (labeled "The Freeman Collection") that she has assembled during decades of compulsive shopping trips to exotic ports on formal cruise ships such as Cunard's QE2, on which she is a regular.

This trip to Never-Never Veraland started when she left her native Montana for Hollywood sometime before World War II. But instead of finding fame and stardom as a chorus girl, she fell in love with the wealthy "Doc" Freeman, known then as the "Optometrist to the stars." Eventually, they left Hollywood for the cruising life aboard large, crewed motor yachts—all of them named the "White Sands." During one of these cruises in the early 1950s they discovered, and fell in love with, beautiful St. Leonard Creek. They bought hundreds of acres, filled in a shoreline with tons of white sand (all long since washed away), opened a private marina and clubhouse, and called it the White Sands Yacht Club.

For years, it was a "must" stop along the follow-the-sun, cruising circuit of large motor yachts. But nearby Solomons, once nothing but a fishing village, is much closer to the Chesapeake Bay and has developed into a major pleasure boating center. The luxury-boat traffic in Veraland slowed down considerably, although Vera endures as a living legend.

How long will it all last? Species like Vera may seem as if they'll go on forever, but the fact is they will not. What would she do if she retired or sold out? "It's true I travel from October to April," she says, "but I don't know what I would do if I didn't have this restaurant to come back to in the spring. Oh, let's not talk about such unpleasant things. It's much too depressing. Let's just have another cocktail and have some more fun!"

Miss Annie, the Troll Lady, Annapolis ⌒

There is no bridge quite like the Weems Creek swing bridge in Annapolis and no bridgetender quite like "Miss Annie" Bellinger, 71, whose concealed tender's cabin is the only one in the state tucked under the bridge rather than on top of it.

Only three Maryland roadway bridges open for boat traffic by a section of the bridge being swung to the side rather than being raised vertically. This 100-foot-long span connects the Ridgely Avenue shorelines and provides a pleasant short cut for locals who are not in too much of a hurry, or, in some cases, are in too much of a hurry. Viewed from the nearby Rowe Boulevard overpass, the Weems Creek bridge appears to be out of another era, nestled snugly in a sylvan glade.

Annapolitans seem to like their old fashioned bridges, judging from all the commotion raised over the replacement of the old Severn River drawbridge, just around the corner from Annie's span. The one other drawbridge in Annapolis crosses Spa Creek, and during the boating season is far busier than Annie's.

"I'm here from the end of May until the end of October, from dawn to dusk, seven days a week," says Annie, whose plywood deck adjoining the bridgetender's cabin under the roadway is furnished with a few old chairs and folding cushions. This great grandmother has been on the job here for eleven years. "Before I came, the roadway had wooden planks and the bridge had to be cranked open by hand," she says. "Now we're automated and all I have to do is climb up to the roadway, walk out to the middle of the bridge, unlock a control box and press one button to lower the road gates and another button to open the bridge."

She serves about thirty boats docked up the creek and springs to action at a blast of a boat horn. "I have a phone here and sometimes they'll call first," she adds. "If boaters say they won't be returning until later at night, I wait until they come back, even if it's one o'clock in the morning. It's part of the bridgetender's job."

Annie has four dogs to keep her company: Teddy Bear, Nicky, Murphy, and Gizmo. She walks to work with them from her house, about two miles away, and takes them for rides in her small dinghy, paddling around the creek to pick up trash and floating logs. Sometimes she will row the short distance out to the Sev-

ern River when boating activity is slow, but she always listens for those who signal for the bridge to be opened.

During a busy day she may open the bridge twenty-five times, taking about ten minutes for each opening. "Some motorists don't like it," she says, "but most take advantage of the break, get out of their cars, and watch and ask me questions. I call myself the Troll because I 'live' under the bridge. Some think this is actually my home."

Annie has put in a low bid each year for the job, and in 1992 was paid $11,400. Paying her is more economical than building a new, fixed bridge. The current span replaced an old wooden bridge in the early 1950s, but it hasn't been painted in fifteen years and may eventually be updated by a hydraulic bascule (lift) opening system. "Who knows?" she says. "Maybe they'll decide to just tear it down and reroute traffic over the Rowe Boulevard bridge," which is a stone's throw upstream from Annie's bridge.

There are 2,200 state highway bridges in Maryland. The only other remaining swing spans are the Route 231 Benedict bridge, spanning the upper Patuxent River, and the Route 331 Dover bridge crossing the upper Choptank River, east of Easton.

It may seem as if Annie has had a boring life, but it has been anything but. She grew up in a big house in Waterbury, Connecticut, and fell into a kind of nomadic routine when she married first a military man and then a carnival worker. She once frolicked as a "mermaid" in a traveling carny show. She got into the bridgetending business in the Florida Keys, where she was also a bartender.

Now Annie Bellinger has settled into a routine fit for someone with six children, eleven grandchildren, and eleven great-grandchildren. Her mermaiding days are long over. Her grandchildren like nothing better than to visit with her under the bridge and watch her in action. How many other grandchildren can say they have a troll for a grandmother?

Carlton Rhoderick, Linotype Man, Middletown ∾

My search to find a small newspaper plant in Maryland regularly using an outmoded hot lead linotype machine to set news type came to a sudden end in the summer of 1991 in Middletown. I caught Carlton Rhoderick, 70, setting type for what was to be the last edition of the 146-year-old *Valley Register* in the Middletown Valley, west of Frederick.

Traditionally, a newspaper publisher saves that final, sad farewell story announcing the folding of a publication until the last minute, hand-carrying the secret copy to the pressroom. This has nothing to do with sentiment. It is to pull the last possible dollar from advertisements. One would have thought that Rhoderick, a former owner and the only typesetter left at the Middletown weekly, would have known what was going on. "I didn't have a clue while setting the type for the last page one lead story ["Area Graduates at Hood College"] in that final May 31 issue of eight pages," he said. Here he was, participating in the last rites marking the passing of his own profession and he didn't even know it was happening.

By the winter of 1993, the old *Valley Register* building at 123 West Main Street was being converted by Rhoderick into apartments and offices—another renovation in a charming, rediscovered Frederick County town being surrounded by suburban development and bedroom communities. The *Valley Register* sign out front is gone, but the sweet smell of printer's ink still permeates the first floor of the old-fashioned building where four antique linotype machines stood side by side on concrete slabs on reinforced, bare wooden floors. The only newspaper artifacts left are in a back room—a nineteen-ton flatbed Babcock press, a ponderous industrial dinosaur from the early 1900s, and twenty tons of lead "pigs" used for making the type.

"The linotypes went to Mexico," said Rhoderick, pointing out the empty slabs where they had stood for decades. "I don't what's going to happen to this old press. My God! You wouldn't believe the racket this thing made. It used to take us forty-five minutes to print a thousand pages.

When the *Valley Register's* last pressman had a stroke and died, John Saxon, the new publisher, who bought the paper from Rhoderick in 1985, tried to run the

Babcock. "He wasn't very good at it," says the semi-retired Rhoderick, who is also a pressman. Rhoderick continued to set the type for the paper "as a favor," because no one else was efficient at it. "I told the new owner he should modernize and go offset, but it didn't happen," he added. "It was getting more and more difficult to get printers, pressmen, and linotype operators because there were no more technical schools turning them out. Besides, computers had taken over anyway."

Ottmar Mergenthaler, of Baltimore, changed the technology of printing when he invented the "line o' type" in 1885. He tried to sell his first machine to his hometown paper, the Baltimore *Sun*, but the publishers weren't interested. The new technology allowed one man to do the work of eight; the very same thing that happened when computers threw the linotype men out of work.

Once, when Carlton's father, George C. Rhoderick, Jr., owned the paper, the *Register* had two shifts and six linotype men. Carlton, who later became a vice president and publisher, also did reporting, rewriting, layout, photography, copy editing and was managing editor, as well as a typesetter, occasional pressman, and all-around mechanic and carpenter.

They published three weeklies and were jobbers for other independent publications. In addition, they printed ten school newspapers and had nearly two dozen people on the payroll. "We had deadlines every day," Rhoderick says. "I remember going out to cover stories and coming back to actually write them on the linotype!"

Operating a linotype was a curious job in many ways. Linotype operators had to watch out for splatterings of the hot lead, heated to 550 degrees, that could burn off the skin. Also, they had to be proficient at reading copy upside down and fast.

"If it wasn't for this old Babcock press, you wouldn't even know there was a newspaper published here," observes Rhoderick, as he installs three modern hot water heaters right in front of the mammoth machine, which would look right at home in a museum.

Miss Marguerite, Tea Room Waitress, Baltimore ⌒

The last social link to a bygone era of grand department stores and upscale specialty shops, which once attracted shoppers to downtown Baltimore, survives at 333 N. Charles Street in a gentle tea room where time has stood still for 111 years. The unhurried Woman's Industrial Exchange does not accept change lightly and, indeed, has an alert, all-female governing committee that traditionally guards against it. A black doorman, wearing white cotton gloves, sits on a high stool by the vestibule door. Inside, a quiet air of feminine gentility is maintained in a surrounding of homemade cakes and cookies sold side by side with handmade, ruffled smocks for "smart" little girls.

While the afternoon high tea, once frequented by small groups of chauffeured matrons in hats and gloves, is now a thing of the past, one tradition survives in the dominating if diminutive "Miss Marguerite," chief waitress.

Having waited on people in downtown lunch and tea rooms for more than seventy-five years, Marguerite Schertle is a dynamo. Tending tables in the front part of the main dining room, at the remarkable age of 92, she lords over everything. She began working at the Exchange a mere forty-five years ago after spending two decades at the now-closed Dutch Tea Room across the street and another decade at the Lovely Lane Lunch Room.

"I remember serving Wallis Warfield Simpson and her Aunt Bessie," says the active redhead who wears stylish, oversize eyeglasses and sensible white shoes. Wallis Warfield Simpson, of course, was the Belle of Biddle Street, the late Duchess of Windsor, whose husband, Edward VIII, had abdicated the British throne for, he said, "The woman I love." Other customers have included actresses Katharine Hepburn, Julie Harris, Celeste Holm, Sandy Dennis, Jessica Tandy, and Colleen Dewhurst.

"In the old days, a waitress carrying a tray here was considered undignified. We had girls to do that and bus the tables," says Miss Marguerite. "Now we do everything ourselves. Times have changed, even here." But waitresses still wear white sashes (not aprons) tied around their waists with huge bows in the back.

The menu has changed somewhat, too, although items such as chicken croquettes still show up as specials. Kidney and giblet stews and pies have disap-

peared, but white meat chicken salad, crab cakes, and softshell crabs are still on hand. The standard desserts also flourish: butterscotch and lemon tarts, charlotte russe, floating island, and homemade bittersweet chocolate sauce and real whipped cream. Dorothea Day Wilson, one of the cooks, "has been here since she was 16, and she makes everything from scratch," says Miss Marguerite, who has helped in the kitchen, too. "Salad dressings, mayonnaise, corn muffins, buckwheat cakes, you name it—all from scratch."

There is a tradition of sisters working here. Miss Marguerite and her twin sister, the late "Miss Anna" Schertle (who died in 1992), waited tables together for many decades. They also married look-alike brothers, Charles and William, who took turns driving them downtown to work. They even lived next door to one another in look-alike Cape Cod bungalows in Hamilton.

Two other sisters are waitresses at the Exchange: Carrie Geraghty and Loretta Tarbert, who also worked together at the Hochschild-Kohn tea room at Howard and Lexington streets before that department store closed, along with Hutzler's, Stewart's, and the May Company.

Why is it called the Exchange? Well, it goes back to post–Civil War days, which saw many widows "left impoverished by fate." A wealthy Baltimore woman, Mrs. G. Harmon Brown, set up an "exchange" in her home "for the purpose of endeavoring by sympathy and practical aid to encourage and help needy women in reduced circumstances to help themselves by procuring for them and establishing a salesroom for the sale of women's work protected from a publicity from which a generous nature shuns." Women's handiwork still fills the front room, where a past century awaits visitors.

The doorman sometimes comes outside to help patrons up the worn white marble steps, into a vestibule with a marble-tiled floor and wooden wainscoting, and through double doors of wood and glass with sleigh bells tingling from the doorknob. The high ceiling is sheathed in pressed tin, and ancient wooden-bladed ceiling fans turn slowly over a Victorian wood and glass counter, where a refined manager, Rita Knox, presides elegantly behind a cashier's cage in a bright and sunny room filled with wonderful things.

A mechanical contraption as indecorous as a cash register is not allowed. They use cash drawers with wooden, concave trays, and old-fashioned adding machines. Wilhelmina Godwin, 83, is a sales clerk and a bookkeeper who "keeps the ledgers" —and they are ledgers.

The store has high-quality, handmade items of great delicacy that must meet the "Exchange standards" of being of high value and aiding a deserving woman;

no cutesy, knick-knacky crafts. "Consignees get 65 cents on the dollar," reports Mrs. Knox, a veteran of O'Neill's department store, another classic Baltimore institution gone from downtown. One standard item, especially irresistible to doting grandfathers with granddaughters, is the smock dress for little girls. "We have also sold baptismal dresses, which have been passed down from one generation to another," adds Mrs. Knox.

"The problem we face," she says, "is that our ladies who make this handiwork are elderly. There is no one to do their fine needlework and the almost lost art of knotted colonial muslin bedspreads, for example. One of our ladies has been making this exquisite embroidery for the Exchange for sixty years, and her mother did it before her. There is no one to take her place. All these items are vanishing because no one does this work anymore."

The Exchange continues to operate as it did when it was incorporated in 1882 by a group of socially prominent women, following a trend that started in Philadelphia and spread to other cities. Baltimore's exchange is one of the oldest with a tea room and a consignment shop. In 1887 the women bought the elegant, 3½-story building with the Flemish bond brick, which is now listed on the National Register of Historic Places. The circa 1815 structure was once a rooming house, with an addition on the rear, but it retains much of its early-nineteenth-century townhouse character.

Downstairs is the "Down Under" restaurant (where smoking is permitted), seating about fifteen around a U-shaped counter, originally established for men. But even the upstairs dining room, with its marble fireplaces and fluted cast-iron columns, is unisex now. The big dining room has a hand-painted mural of old Baltimore, a black-and-white checkered linoleum floor, and seats a hundred. It is open only for breakfast and lunch and is the preferred room for most ladies of the Exchange who don't smoke.

"I don't know what I'd do with myself if I didn't work here," says Miss Marguerite, who may well be the oldest full-time waitress in Maryland. "We know all our regular customers by their first names, calling them 'Miss This' and 'Miss That.' It's like a family. My customers remember my birthday, and I try to remember their birthdays. We're always passing around pictures of our grandchildren and great-grandchildren."

If Miss Marguerite occasionally forgets a name, she rarely forgets a face. "I remember staring at a middle-aged woman having lunch with her grown daughters and asking if she came here as a little girl with her mother and grandmother. She said, 'Oh, Miss Marguerite, I never thought you would remember!' But I did.

It was a very happy occasion." They represented a third and fourth generation that Marguerite Schertle had served, and she is looking forward to a fifth generation of the same family coming for the chicken salad and the charlotte russe.

"I hope I'm still working here when I turn 100, and if I can't work here I hope I can at least come for lunch!" she laughed, swirling around and spinning on a dime then dashing off to the kitchen for seconds on the chocolate sauce for one of her regulars who really didn't need it.

Bill's Place, Little Orleans ~

Hikers, campers, boaters, canoeists, bicyclists, fishermen, hunters, motorcycle gangs, lost tourists—they all find their way at one time or another to Bill's Place in Little Orleans, an isolated Allegany County oasis and once a stopping point for Chesapeake and Ohio Canal barges and Western Maryland Railway freight train crews. Located along Orleans Road at the far southeastern edge of the 38,000-acre Green Ridge State Forest, it looks like a stagecoach or pony express outpost. The nearest settlements are miles away on the other side of the Potomac River, in West Virginia, at Paw Paw and Great Cacapon.

"That's just the way I like it: old-timey and not about to change," says proprietor Bill Schoenadel, 70. "I've had three generations of scouts from the same family in here, and the next generation will recognize it when they come in with the first, as long as I'm here."

A smoker of el cheapo cigars, he goes through fifty a week. On his battered swinging front doors is a sign reading "Mayor's Office" that someone stole and posted because he is known as the mayor of Little Orleans. It is a town with one store, one church, and an early-nineteenth-century graveyard with some old tombstones that bear only birthdates, as if still waiting for those people to die.

The canal that put Little Orleans on the map is now a 185-mile national historic towpath park for hikers, who walk the very paths once used by the barge-towing mules, who hit speeds of two miles per hour. The last freight train rumbled through town in 1978, but the Little Orleans store, established in 1832, survives. The in-house post office is gone, along with the blacksmith and wheelwright shops, which vanished with the departure of horse and wagon transportation.

The structure that is Bill's Place was originally on Cresap's Trail (the National Pike) and was moved one hundred yards in 1904 to make room for the railroad. The creaky wooden porch with two fragile swings has porch railings where an occasional horseman ties up to water his mount and himself. One may even encounter men wearing pistol belts and carrying rifles—all of them wearing caps and boots. This place is a mecca for deer hunters; hunting licenses are sold and bagged deer are checked in. During the one-week season in early December Bill's

Place can go five days without closing. In 1992 they registered 176 deer. The decidedly Old West atmosphere is encouraged by Bill's leave-it-as-it-is policy.

Inside, there is a whole other story. In the spring, summer, and autumn the place is often booming with outdoor types buying field supplies. There are two pool tables, an upright piano, eight video game machines, and live music, when the right combination of pickers and fiddlers shows up to foot stomp into the night. There is also a jukebox in the "recreation room."

During the summer, Bill maintains a fleet of twenty-eight rental canoes. A retired printer, he bought the establishment in 1968, and he still does some commercial printing in the basement on an 1892 press. He tends bar and waits tables, with a little help from his wife, Ethel, some of his five children, and his friends. Homemade signs hang all over the place, most of them signed "Bill." They read: "Children Must be Seated at all Times," "All Minors Must be Out by 9 p.m.," "Shirts Required in Pool Room," "You Must Play Only One (pool) Table at a Time: Give Other Peoples a Chance to Play," "Closed for Fishing at Any Time," "Please Put Cigarettes in the Ash-Tray's," "This is Not Burger King: You get it Our Way or You Don't Get the son-of-a-bitch at All!"

His bar is stocked with large jars of pickles, pig's feet, and Polish sausage. There are two rest rooms, both of them "unisex." He sells bait, groceries, beer, wine, firewood, ice, sandwiches, T-bone steaks and meatloaf with mashed potatoes. Heating is by a kerosene stove.

Posted on the walls are color snapshots documenting memorable parties, more signs, and attached to the ceiling are 6,000 dollar bills, signed by their donors from forty-two states, and foreign currency from fifteen countries, many bearing scribbled messages. Bill lives above the store, with a hunter's arsenal within easy reach. He has ledgers dating to the early 1900s that were kept by one C. T. Callen, who sold sugar (25 pounds for $1.63), calico (six yards for 42 cents), nails (five pounds for 15 cents), even furniture.

"You'll look long and hard, but you won't find another place anything like this place, I can tell you that," says Bill through a haze of cigar smoke. "And no," he adds, "we do not have a no-smoking section in our dining room. If you don't want to smoke, you can go outside and not do it."

Cutts & Case, Wooden Yacht Builders, Oxford ⌒

There are boatyards and there are boatyards on the Chesapeake Bay. "Real" boat-yards—where wooden pleasure yachts are planned, designed, built, repaired, restored, maintained, stored, docked, appreciated, and loved—are a disappearing rarity. But at the Cutts and Case Boatyard in Oxford, boat-loving builder Ed Cutts, 66, has been carrying on a family tradition of boatbuilding in America that dates from 1646, although he has been at it in Oxford only since 1965, a time when fiberglass began displacing wood as a boatbuilding material.

Approaching the yard by land on an oyster shell road, one is greeted by an engaging sign, in a sweet wooded grove, proclaiming "Cutts and Case, Where Neptune's Darlings Gather." These "darlings," however, are best observed in their natural habitat, which calls for approaching the yard very slowly by boat via Town Creek.

It is an idyllic location that attracts painters, photographers, and picnickers; a place for strollers and idlers, where there are no locked doors, high chainlink fences, or "No Trespassing" signs. Perhaps this is because Ed and Maggie Cutts live here as well as work here. The boatyard torments real estate developers in upscale Oxford, a sailing center and haven for wealthy retirees, where even small homes sell in the $300,000 range. The yard, however, just adds to the 300-year-old charm of what may be the loveliest village on the Eastern Shore.

The yard's distinctive dark red wooden boatsheds, with white trim and slanted tin roofs, harken back to the 1920s when famed boatbuilder Ralph Wiley ran a first-class operation here, just beyond the Tred Avon River entrance to the quiet town harbor. It was a stroke of luck that Ed Cutts, the late John Case, and Ralph Wiley found one another. It is not often that one great boatyard is succeeded by another. Many a buyer would have barged in there, bulldozed the trees and the sheds, enlarged the marina and soon had the property looking like a shopping mall parking lot, with "boatels" filled with plastic brokerage boats.

Some visitors mistake the yard for a museum because of all the elegant wood-en yachts in residence, but Cutts has patented a modern procedure, called the Cutts method, for building strong, high-grade, lightweight, roomy wooden yachts in a double-planking process using Kevlar cord stringings set in epoxy. He still

works primarily in wood, only using the synthetic materials to make the wood long-lasting. He sides with his mentor, famed yacht designer L. Francis Herreshoff, when it comes to "building boats out of a pot." Herreshoff called fiberglass "frozen snot."

Cutts does not call his yard a marina, even though boats are docked there. He has no showers, snack bar, cocktail lounge, swimming pool, putt-putt golf course, or fuel pumps. It's a boatyard, pure and simple. He hauls his boats out of the water by two methods: a crane on tractor treads set up by the water's edge, and on an old marine railway.

Two Cutts sons work at the yard—Ed Jr., 37, and Ronald, 32. Ed Sr. is proud of the fact he has never laid off a worker, and he has a curious traditional approach to evaluating them. "An employee must have an ethically sound quality about him," he told one local boating writer. "I can't teach him to be a good person. If he's a no-good person, then he'll know how to change part of a degree with a plane, but he'll still not be a good person. Therefore, the quality of everything he does will always be in question."

Cutts is a designer, innovator, inventor, and romantic dreamer who is incapable of building an ugly boat. "His sailboats are low-profiled and lithe-slender, with flowing curves," said yachting writer Roger Vaughn, of Oxford. "The [steering] wheels he puts on boats are wood, but they are also horizontal, easier on the back, he says, and they double as cockpit tables."

The yard is a delightful place for poking around, especially for anyone interested in wooden boats that are just lovely to look at, in or out of water. In one very large shed, small and large boats are on view as if in a prearranged display, only they are here to be worked on. A potbellied coal stove warms the workshed, where something is always going on and no one is chased away because of worries about insurance regulations. There is a lure here that draws people interested in old boating ways, using old tools and for all the right reasons.

How long this place can survive is anyone's guess. The early 1990s have been particularly hard on the boatbuilding business, and Cutts has taken his financial hits along with others, although you wouldn't know it by listening to him. Cutts, you see, is haunted by the grandeur and tradition of maintaining the legendary high quality of yards in New York and New Jersey: Phyfe's, the Purdy Brothers, and Nevins, a boatbuilder's nirvana that closed in the late 1950s. Cutts learned his trade working in some of these yards.

Listen to him talk about the amazing deeds of the Nevins crew from Nova Scotia:

I saw one man, Adolf Trahan, put the fashion piece in a yacht's transom and double-plank it all in one day. The fashion piece was so perfect the planks didn't need to be trimmed at all. It was the best work I ever saw. That sort of craftsmanship was going on all the time, and those guys took it for granted. They weren't boaters themselves. They wanted to go home after work and plant tomatoes. . . . The problem today is that we don't have any artisans. There's no work ethic. People would rather trot down the road in an expensive outfit with their mind turned off.

But in Oxford we still have the high-grade boatyard of Ed Cutts. For now, at least. Let's hope it lasts, or at least hope for another successor to follow in the gentle wake of Wiley, Cutts, and Case.

Baltimore's Last Cannery, Canton ⌒

Shouts of "Tomato truck! Tomato truck!" from youths looking for a free tomato or two are heard no more in Baltimore's ethnic neighborhoods. The tomato-laden trucks headed for canneries along Canton's Cannery Row are gone, as are the canneries, in a city that was once the nation's leading canner of fruits and vegetables. Also gone are the can factories that supplied those canneries.

Many of the factories and warehouses along East Baltimore's waterfront have been converted into condos, which leaves Mike Manning, 70—the operator of the city's last cannery—pondering the fate of his family's hominy factory in Canton. It has, after all, a sweeping view of rooftops and the harbor in the distance, and there's always a breeze on the upper level. "Who knows?" he muses. "This, too could be a condo one day."

The Manning family entered the canning business when Mike's German immigrant grandmother, Margaret Manning, started a home-canning cottage business in 1904 out of her Canton row house. She sold hominy to neighbors, and then to the ubiquitous corner grocery stores, which also have mostly disappeared, or been converted into guarded fortresses.

In 1917, Mike and Margaret Manning went into the cannery business in a serious way, buying a former slaughter- and smokehouse at 803 South Clinton Street for $5,000. The Manning family continues the hominy-canning tradition, employing about eighteen workers to turn out 10,000 cans of pearly-white hominy every day—wrapped in the distinctive red, white and blue Manning label.

Located in a blue-collar neighborhood surrounded by Catholic churches serving German, Polish, and Irish parishes, the factory takes up a quarter of a city block. Workers have often lived within walking distance of their work. The heart of the cannery is the second floor production room, an operation out of the 1930s dominated by twenty gigantic pressure cookers. It's a noisy place because of all the cans moving about on various automated assembly lines. The bulky machinery is old, but it does the job, "so why fix it or replace it?" asks Manning.

One very important function in this old-fashioned operation takes place in a small room where about ten women, wearing hairnets, sit on stools in front of conveyor belts. Alternating this task with other jobs, they pick out the unworthy

corn kernels from the millions rolling by. One woman, Viola Skahill, has been selecting the pearly whites (Manning Hominy trademarks) for fifty-one years.

"Machines can't do this critical job as well as people, it's as simple as that," says Mike Manning, president and "chief floor sweeper" of M. Manning, Inc. He used to play in the family factory as a child, cooling off in the hot Baltimore summers by hanging on the insides of the cold water tubs that cooled the cans. He went into the business full time after serving in World War II. A low-key, pipe-smoking man with a sense of humor and fairness, Manning is a pack rat who refuses to throw out anything. Working with him is his brother John, 65 (shipping and receiving), and sister Lena, the bookkeeper and the entire payroll department. Among them, they embody nearly 150 years of service.

The front office is a narrow, classic wood-paneled office with a high ceiling and worn wooden desks that appear to have been jammed into place permanently decades ago and never moved. There is one manual typewriter, an old electric adding machine, metal file cabinets, and not a computer in sight. "Miss Lena," as she is known, works behind an old-fashioned glass "pay window" with a half-moon entry cut out at the base. She still stuffs pay envelopes with cash, although employees are now required to sign their pay stubs.

Posted over the time clock is a curious sign stating: "No Cash Advances on Tuesdays and Thursdays." In her very soft and shy voice, Miss Lena smiles sweetly and explains this notice. "We used to give cash advances of $20 or what-have-you with an I.O.U. at any time and just deducted it [without interest] from the next pay," she says. "But it got rather complicated and we had to cut back a bit." They don't go for radical changes at Manning's.

This is an unobtrusive time capsule, emitting a neutral fragrance from its high smokestack. It seems curious that many people don't even know there's a cannery here, in the middle of a residential neighborhood. In fact, it's a last bit of living, working history.

Tubby's Bar, South Baltimore ⌒

One occupation that shows no sign of diminishing in Baltimore is that of neighborhood saloonkeeper, a socially demanding position of trust that requires patience, endurance, and at least some degree of amiability. Most of these public houses welcome strangers, but in close-knit, working-class neighborhoods it is not unusual for interlopers to be greeted with silent, almost hostile stares filled with suspicion and mistrust.

Such a private public place is Tubby's, in the Cross Street Market community of South Baltimore, a tough, hardscrabble part of town with old-fashioned ways. The neighborhood is being swept by a rolling tide of residential and commercial gentrification that has converted some of its bars into places of clean, trendy gentility.

Not so at the house of Tubby, 27 East Cross Street. A unique drinking establishment, it is an endangered commercial environment, operated like a club for the benefit of Tubby (Albert Clayland) and his buddies, some of whom have been coming here for many years and have developed proprietary feelings about the place. This is entirely understandable, because four of these regulars (known as "the heirs") will inherit the two-story building and all its contents upon the demise of Tubby.

The youngest heir is Sal Scardina, 53, the Baltimore City cop on the beat. The others are John Koch, 65, a retired cop; James MacKenzie, 65, a retired railroader; and Tom Carney, 79, a retired IRS agent, Tubby's bookkeeper, and a former schoolmate at St. Mary's Star of the Sea in South Baltimore. Carney calls Tubby "Albert." The heirs have no inclination to run the bar, so it is highly unlikely that Tubby's will continue to exist in its present time-capsule state much longer. And South Baltimore will be the poorer for it.

Tubby, 80, who has tended bar here for the better part of sixty years, is now wheelchair-bound and his eyesight is failing. No longer tubby, he sits in an old theater seat against a totally barren, lime-green wall across from his bar countertop, built in the early 1950s. There is a tabletop black-and-white television on a table to his right, inches from his failing eyes, and an old stereo to his left with stacks of Big Band 33⅓ RPM records. Strapped to his thin right ankle is a holster with a fully loaded, snub-nosed .38 revolver.

"Who's that?" Tubby barks when hearing someone walking in the front door of his saloon, which displays no identifying marks whatever to the curious passer-by. The storefront window is decorated with a row of miniature American flags faded by the sun. Tubby's buddies—who fetch and pay for their own drinks and ring up the odd additional sale on the old cash register—call out names of visitors to put Tubby at ease. They usually sit around on bar stools drinking long-necks, bottles of beer that sell for one dollar. A shot of cheap whiskey also goes for a dollar.

If no buddies have arrived and a stranger walks in, Tubby will announce in his gruff manner that his barmaid didn't show up and the joint is closed. But when the heirs come in, as they do daily, Tubby visibly cheers up and begins spinning Homeric tales of his raucous and romantic ways with the women, exploits that are somewhat ongoing to this day, although not much romance is involved. He is a bit rough around the edges, and his yarns are not for the timid.

Occupying a position of honor, in a gilt frame in the center of the back bar amidst a row of bottles, is a color photograph of the love of his life, the late Betty Bell. She died a decade or so ago, but Tubby still gets weepy when he thinks about her and will order "two birdbaths" (two $1.20 shots of his best whiskey) to console himself. The memory prompts more tales of the bawdy good old days that began when his mother, Elizabeth Kearns, opened the bar "the day Prohibition ended" and ran it as "Ma Kearn's."

Other than shooting the breeze with his buddies, one of Tubby's prime enjoyments is playing pitch (a card game) at the front of the bar, known affectionately as "the Lounge," in a padded red booth with toss cushions oozing foam rubber. "I'm the best goddam pitch player in South Baltimore," boasts the not very humble Tubby, holding cards an inch from his eyes. He has been known to place a wager or two in his long, colorful life. His buddies, of course, agree, especially the four heirs. Tubby's last will and testament once instructed that the saloon would go to the buddy who held the winning hand in one post-mortem game of pitch.

Tubby's hours are anywhere from late morning to mid-afternoon, depending upon his whim and on the comings and goings of his loyal buddies. When the heirs leave, locking the front door behind them, Tubby climbs back upstairs to his apartment above the bar, pulling himself up backwards, step by step. The place takes on an abandoned look. But that's how it often looks anyway.

Hull Street Federal, Maryland's Smallest Bank, South Baltimore ⌒

Some Baltimore building and loans are the stuff of legend, right out of Hollywood's *It's a Wonderful Life* movie classic of 1946, in which George Bailey (Jimmy Stewart) dramatically rescues Bailey's Building and Loan in a crisis, in the process saving his community and his own soul. Maryland's savings and loan association could have used more Baileys during the mid-1980s when many of those institutions got into trouble and went under.

The neighborhood building and loan association was a highly visible, fortress-like stalwart for decades until larger banks began gobbling them up. Some old mom-and-pops are still out there, although their number is diminishing. But Locust Point's old Hull Street Building and Loan—now federally chartered and FDIC-insured as Hull Federal Savings Bank—even survived the Depression. The state's smallest bank, with assets in early 1993 of just $5.5 million, it has been a sound financial institution in its working-class row house neighborhood since opening in 1911.

This may be the only bank in the nation open, more or less for banker's hours, nearly every day of the year, even though the Feds flinch at this idea. But that's the way it goes at 1248 Hull Street, at least for the past several years. Wilbur Baumann, financial secretary and a member of the board of directors, likes to do some things in his own stubbornly unique way, which means being open informally more than any other bank.

From 1911 to 1989, this small storefront bank opened only on Tuesday evenings, because this was the most convenient time for its neighborhood customers, many of whom purchased their homes through the trusted building and loan. But after these small banks were federally chartered in 1989, they were required to open five days a week, from 9 a.m. to 2 p.m. The Hull Street institution, however, has steadfastly retained its Tuesday night hours, purely out of tradition, says Baumann, a Locust Point bachelor who was born in the neighborhood and still lives there.

"This bank is my hobby and I don't know what I'd do without it," he explains. "I'm here a lot, although occasionally we are closed on Christmas Day—if I have somewhere else to go!" he laughs. But if the bank is supposed to be closed and

"Mister Wilbur" is behind the counter (as he often is), he'll just open up when someone knocks on the glass door. He knows all the customers, often by their nicknames. "People I grew up with still call me 'Sticky Buns' because my grandfather was a baker and introduced sticky buns to the neighborhood," he says, laughing.

This bank's operation is unlike any most people have ever seen. There is nothing very modern about it, except for its computers (Baumann bought the bank's first computer a few years ago at a toy store, where a 12-year-old showed him how it worked). He still writes his correspondence on a battered Royal typewriter.

A long, open counter installed in 1950 (no bulletproof-glass tellers' windows here) faces six plain chairs and a bench, separated by a small table with a cooler stored underneath and a small refrigerator stocked with soda pop. There is no air conditioning, but two wooden-bladed ceiling fans and a floor fan at least circulate summer air. Telephones were not installed until 1989, when the Feds said it was required.

On the stuccoed, lime-green walls are faded photocopies of bank documents, informally taped to the wall for public inspection. A church calendar hangs on a nail. A plastic bowl of free Tootsie Rolls is available. Waltz music emerges from a tape deck, perched on a ledge near the old pressed tin ceiling. Nothing fancy about this place.

Tuesday evenings are still conducted like Old Home Nights. Behind the counter are Pauline Lewis, vice president; Raymond Baumann, president; Michael C. Baumann, the bank's attorney; and "Mr. Wilbur," of course. All these Baumanns are related.

Wilbur ("no age, please," he says) must be in his 70s. He has worked here on Tuesday evenings for forty-four years. He is full of complicated, convoluted stories that ramble on and on, about himself and his beloved neighborhood. And he loves to talk about his bank. "We used to sell money orders for 15¢ not very long ago," says Wilbur. "The Feds said that was too low, so now we're all the way up to 35¢. That made them happy, I guess. But then they didn't like the fact that I only drew a $5,000 salary, so we had to raise it to $11,000, even though I don't need that much money."

Karl Ballwanz, 71, has been a customer for fifty years. His neighborhood home was financed here, as was his father's and his two daughters' homes. "I got my mortgage on a handshake," he says. "My payments were $4 a month."

Every Tuesday evening, he brings in nine savings passbooks, each one made out in a different grandchild's name, and deposits something to each account. "I do all my banking here." he says, "and if they had checking I'd do that here, too."

The bank was started by William Mattheiss, who was in the plumbing business. He also loaned money to the local stevedores—50¢ a week, 5¢ interest. He built row houses in Locust Point in the 1920s and 1930s, and his bank came in handy to finance and mortgage them. Mattheiss died in 1942, and his son Karl (Wilbur's second cousin) took over.

The association has always been safe and profitable, and in early 1993 was paying dividends of 6.23 percent on passbook savings accounts (minimum balance $25). "But leave that out!" says Wilbur. "We don't want to get too big for our britches!"

Wilbur pays utility bills for some of his older patrons (with their funds, of course). He also cashes their Social Security checks and personally delivers the cash to those unable to get to the bank. No extra charge. He just does it.

"If I didn't have this bank, I'd go nuts," says Wilbur, who also gives piano lessons and does tax returns on the side. "I love this little bank, and working with numbers. I respect and honor its tradition and history, and I love and honor the people we serve. It's just a heck of a lot of fun!"

G. Krug & Son, Baltimore's Ornamental Iron Craftsmen ⌒

In a visibly depressed area of downtown Baltimore—where the city's great department stores once thrived side by side, luring throngs of shoppers on crowded trolleys and buses—there is now a shopping wasteland. Stores like Hutzler's and Stewart's, along with their thousands of shoppers, are all gone, although a modern commuter light rail, hauntingly trolley-like in appearance, now rolls up and down Howard Street.

Through all this social, industrial, and business upheaval and change, however, one central downtown industry from another age has, remarkably, survived almost intact in the 400 block of West Saratoga Street. G. Krug and Son, ornamental iron craftsmen and blacksmiths, is a working anachronism that wants no part of being a museum, although it is now a national registered landmark.

Curiously, the handsome red brick structure resembles some kind of restoration with a historical plaque by its massive iron door, which one must heave to open. Many driving by think of it as a quaint, sentimental skeleton of a bygone way of life, preserved in all its antiquity with nothing inside. But quaint it ain't. Even though custom ornamental ironworking is vanishing, the old-fashioned work of Krug is going on inside these walls much as it has since 1810, when its neighboring farmers and farm animals strolled by casually.

During Krug's prime years, soon after the Civil War and before World War I, more than thirty German artisans labored here to bedeck the city in heavy but graceful ornamentation: iron window boxes, doors, fences, gates, hardware. They also added elegant touches to buildings with cast iron fronts. These aristocrats of labor arrived for work driving two-horse buggies and wearing tall silk hats.

Today, what was dismantled during patriotic scrap drives during World War II and later discarded in favor of "modernization," is being replaced. But it's not entirely for romantic reasons. The current demand for ornamental ironwork that has rejuvenated Krug and Son in the years since 1970 has been for protective grills for reasons of security.

Krug's current president, bearded Stephen Krug, 37, is a pragmatist with a deep sense of history who is not at home at the blacksmith's forge. He leaves that work to his skilled blacksmith brother, Peter, 31, who is very much at home there.

"It's a feeling hard to describe," Stephen once said, "but my great-great-grandfather, my great-grandfather, my grandfather, and my father worked here." When he says this, there is a burden lurking deep in his eyes. In draftsmen's drawers above his office are his ancestors' beautiful ink drawings on linen paper, samples of the delicate work done here, and the very tools and equipment they used.

"I drive around this city and constantly come face to face with the work of my ancestors," he says. It must be a terribly intimidating reminder that, somehow, he is expected to continue their work and maintain the high level of this disappearing craftsmanship.

There is much he would like to find out about the building which is now his inheritance. "That this was close to being razed by the city for the kind of high-rise parking lot towering behind us is almost impossible to comprehend," he says. "But my father (Theodore Krug) fought long and hard to save it, and save it he did."

The history of the place goes back to 1810 when one Augustus Schwatka established a blacksmith operation here. Between 1830 and 1870 it was owned by A. Merker, who brought in the first Krug (Gustav) as his partner. Merker lived above his shop, and the tattered remains of his wallpaper still hang in his bedrooms, now used for storage.

"Our work is 70 percent specialty and 30 percent security bar and grill work," says Stephen Krug. "But we can reproduce all our old work from original drawings, which are beautiful just to look at. We don't 'stock' anything, as such. It's all one-of-a-kind work that will last, we hope, forever."

Only three skilled metal craftsmen work in the wonderful street level shop that is something out of another age. Little has changed, and even the front office where Krug and draftsman Warren Miller work has retained a nineteenth-century look. They also retain the quirks and the inventive gimmicks, even little cubbyhole hideaway rooms.

"Look at all these drawers that go all the way to the ceiling," says Krug, getting on his knees to closely decipher the faded, ornate penmanship labeling the contents. "I don't even know what's in all these drawers! It's probably full of stuff that we don't even use anymore, but how can I throw it out? Look at this old business card," he says, handing over a card ornamented by an intricate spider-webbed fence flanked by two wind vanes. It reads: "G. Krug & Son, manufacturers of every description of wrought and cast iron work, railing, shutters, doors, balconies, verandahs, cresting, vanes, finials, builders' iron work, &c."

John Smith's Barbershop, Lonaconing ⌐⌐

Of all the time capsule professions still flourishing in Maryland, among the most numerous and most resistant to change is the neighborhood barbershop. Competition from unisex styling salons threatens these tonsorial museums, which often function with one or two white porcelain Koken barber chairs and a lone barber— usually older and balding—circling a usually older and balding male patron with scissors flying and hair clippers buzzing.

Some of these barbers worked for their barbering fathers and grandfathers and have been cutting hair the same way, and in the same parlors, for sixty or seventy years. Some even live above the shop. They scoff at using blow-dryers or raising prices much above $6.

John Smith's Barbershop opened in Lonaconing in 1870 and has been at its current location for 106 years, in a little shoebox of a building set on stilts over George's Creek. It is the only barbershop left in this economically depressed Allegany County town. And Burton Smith, 69, is the last Smith to be barbering in a barbering family that goes back five generations to Scotland.

"I received my master barber's license when I was 10 years old," he says, "but I started working here as a lather and sweep-up boy when I was 4, when my grandfather, John Smith, and my father, John "Judd" Smith and three barbering uncles were all here. Remember, this was a busy town with a population of 10,000. There were seven other barbershops! Now there's just me."

Some customers have been coming here for seventy-five years for the same style haircuts: short on top, short on the sides, short around the back. "I don't do razor cuts or blow-dry styling," he says. For the sideburns, Smith hones his straight edge with a stone, then takes off the edge by stropping it on a leather and canvas strap. "Used to be that when you got a haircut you got a shave, too, and even a shoeshine," he adds. "I still use hot lather and a straight razor for trim, but I haven't had a request for a shave in years and just don't do it anymore. We had three hundred individual shaving mugs here at one time!"

Although it's quiet now, in its day John Smith's Barbershop must have been quite a lively place, although "Granpap" allowed no cursing, drinking or smoking. But he loved music and used to play the concertina with real barbershop quartets, singing coal miners, bagpipers, and Scots reciting the poetry of Robert Burns.

"This used to be community hangout," says Smith. "In fact, we had to separate the loafers from the customers. The loafers went into a back room, behind a partition, because those who wanted a haircut would look in, think there was a long wait, and go to another barbershop."

Today's entertainment is provided by the police and fire radio scanner and the occasional posting of a witticism, such as: "Stress is the confusion created when one's mind overrides the body's basic desire to choke the living hell out of some jackass who desperately needs it."

Smith, a bachelor, says he wouldn't know what to do with himself if he didn't have his barbershop: "I like to keep the place as original looking as possible and I never throw away anything. Antique dealers are always coming in here wanting to buy everything. I don't even tell them about the back room, where all the real old stuff is stored."

Wearing an old-fashioned, double-breasted, white surgical smock that buttons over one shoulder and down the side, Smith cuts hair in a two-chair shop. He calls the 1920-vintage Koken barber chairs, from St. Louis, the "new chairs." The "old chairs," from the 1880s, are in the back room, along with the shop's potbellied stove, oil lamps, and other antique barbering equipment.

A piece that draws a lot of attention is the iron, candy-striped barber pole outside—a late-nineteenth-century tradesman's sign, also from the Koken Company, which turned out thousands of barber chairs that are still in use today throughout the country.

Smith's handsomely ornate, solid oak counter frame—purchased from the J. J. Ryan Barbershop Supply Company in Baltimore in the late 1870s—has three round, built-in, beveled mirrors and a marble counter. Within easy reach is a small sprinkling jug of Witch Hazel brand hair tonic, and a snubby, worn horsehair brush for talcum dusting.

Smith has an early commercial hair dryer, but he just shows it as part of his "working barbershop museum." Ask him to "blow-dry" your hair and, likely as not, he'd pretend to clobber you with it, explaining: "I don't go for that weird stuff."

When the town was booming, John Smith's Barbershop stayed open until 8 p.m. on weekdays and 10:30 p.m. on Saturdays; but the population is down to under 2,000, and the deep coal mines, the glass factory, and the silk mill of Lonaconing are all closed. "I'll keep the barbershop open as long as I need something to do," says Burton Smith, "but when I close, that's the end of it."

The Last Picture Show, Pocomoke City ⌒

Smalltown Maryland's vintage movie houses never seem to quite die, even after the last picture show flickers out. They often function again under other personalities, although a very few have been reborn as theaters after infusions of public funds. The architecturally intact survivors are converted for purposes such as independent churches or mini-malls, but haunting reminders of their former grandeur cling to the upper facades, above modernized street level entrances that attempt to cover up their let's-pretend past.

There is one theater on the Lower Eastern Shore, however, still functioning in its original use and in its original building. It is about the only business left that lights up an otherwise darkened Market Street in Pocomoke City on Friday, Saturday, and Sunday nights. The Mar-Va Theater may not remain open for much longer; for some 8 p.m. showings, not one patron shows up. One of its problems (along with TV and VCRs) is Salisbury, a nearby city gone shopping center–mad, that has all but killed its own central downtown mall to lure the mobile shopper. There are modern theaters at these malls, offering dozens of first-run movies.

What keeps the Mar-Va alive is the sentimental heart of Tom Doub, 50, a weekend commuter from his home in faraway Ellicott City, near Baltimore. A music teacher, he fell in love as a teenager with the theater organ music at downtown Baltimore's grand motion picture palaces—the Stanley, Hippodrome, Town, Keith's, and the Loew's Century and Valencia, all of them now demolished or closed. It had long been his fantasy to have his own theater organ, but one must have a proper place to put such an instrument, preferably some place affordable that offers stage shows and music as well as movies in the format Doub enjoyed so much as a youth. When he heard in 1988 that the Mar-Va was for sale, he bought it.

Today, Doub the theater owner is also Doub the usher, maintenance man, floor sweeper and, on Saturday nights, projectionist, showing second-run movies from his balcony projection booth. A lady friend, Marty Long, sells the tickets and also fills in wherever needed. "Fortunately, I have a sense of humour about all this," says Doub, laughing. "I knew it would be a financial risk, but I just couldn't

54

resist it. But what choice did I have? I had to have a proper home for my theater organ!"

The routine in the past was curious. Traditionally, Friday nights were for white kids, Saturday nights for black kids, and Sunday nights for adults. Now, of course, everyone is welcome at all showings. "We used to show a movie to as few as three people," says Doub, who raised the admission from $2 to $3.50 for everyone. "But we can't even begin to pay for the electricity and heat on three admissions, so we've had to set a policy of having a minimum of eight viewers before we show the movie."

Considering that the 1927-vintage theater has some 700 seats, there is a feeling of forlorn hopelessness when no one shows up. Even so, Doub has installed an 800-pipe Marr and Colton theater pipe organ backstage that he hopes to play one day. Air conditioning, however, is out of the question.

The theater, with its low, overhanging marquee held in place by chains, is a throwback to the late 1930s, when it was last "modernized." Bare light bulbs outline the lower edges of the marquee, and theatrical face masks (representing comedy and tragedy) flank the letters spelling out "MAR-VA" (short for Maryland-Virginia).

A tiny, enclosed ticket booth is at the center of the outer lobby, which is entered through large swinging glass doors. A shiny brass railing for crowd control leads to the curtained ticket window, where the following notice is posted: "The Mar-Va has tried to allow maximum freedom for kids on Friday night. Due to excessive noise and horseplay it is necessary to set limits. If needed, your parents will be called."

The candy-vending machines are gone, but a circa-1946 popcorn dispenser still drops popcorn into a bag for 10¢. Sodas are available in the adjacent "sweet shop," an old fashioned fountain (also owned by Doub).

The aroma inside the theater is unmistakably early movie house Americana; dank and musty, with seedy, threadbare red carpets. Wooden theater seats with curved backs have been "improved" with cushioned seats (some duct-taped), although some unpadded hard seats remain in the front rows.

Now closed is a segregated side entrance that was in use until the mid-1960s. The stairway led to a separate ticket booth where tickets were sold to blacks, who were restricted to a balcony with its own segregated restrooms.

The Mar-Va has an interesting, purely local history. After it opened in December of 1927, John and Lester Fox ran it, before opening the much smaller Fox Theater across the street in the 1940s. J. Dawson Clarke played the piano for the silent movies, on an upright that is there today. He played for vaudeville and minstrel shows, too.

In 1937 the Mar-Va was remodeled and a red carpet installed. The side walls were embossed with gold brocade paneling and the pilasters painted by artists from Philadelphia, who also refinished the pressed-tin ceiling. Small fans lining the walls were replaced with two large built-in air blowers, but the large stage drapes survive and are in operation, exposing a "flying" movie screen that can be hoisted to the rafters. There are dressing rooms on the lower level.

In 1949, Clarke, of Pocomoke City, bought the theater; and his wife, "Miss Hattie," began a forty-year stint in the ticket booth. Also helping out were a daughter, Mrs. Jeanne Byrd (she saw *Gone with the Wind* twenty-four times there), and a long-time family friend, Roger Mariner, a retired rural postman. For eighteen years, Clarke was the town mayor, but his first love was always the Mar-Va, although he recorded only one mildly profitable year while running it. He died in 1986, and Miss Hattie died in 1992.

Doub is following in the tradition of the Clarkes, having agreed to buy the place on the stipulation that it must be used as a theater. He laughs at people who call the Mar-Va a white elephant. "It has been a fantasy of mine that became reality," he says. "I just hope I will not be the one to preside over the last picture show in Pocomoke City."

Hurlock Hardware ⌣

Dusty, dark, and fragrantly smelly hardware stores are familiar fixtures in Maryland, especially in some inner-city Baltimore neighborhoods where someone may be in dire need of something in a hurry to fix some plumbing. But even the hardiest of these stores are changing, at least outwardly, in a tide of modernization calling for new facades, display windows, and plastic signs. It's a survival technique to keep up with the clean, bright, and tidy competition from super shopping mall stores (with hardware departments and uniformed attendants).

While few of these old stores carry the pungent aroma of kerosene, fertilizer, seeds and feed anymore, many still harbor a "Mr. Fixit," the heart and soul of any real community hardware store worth its nuts and bolts. Such gifted, inventive handymen, who have honed their skills in their own home workshops, do more than sell the correct tools and materials for a job. They can demonstrate how to do the job, and they may often do it themselves for the customer in the store's back-room workshop.

Some hardware store owners are reluctant to change and are quite hard-headed about updating their store layouts, mainly because they never have room enough for everything. Good examples of these holdouts are Zeskind's (1890) in West Baltimore, Montgomery County's L. W. White and Son (1880) in Norbeck, and Dorchester County's Hurlock Hardware (1899) in the Upper Eastern Shore town of Hurlock. But there are numerous others hanging in there.

The Hurlock store features an unusual pebble-textured exterior of pressed, galvanized tin sheeting. There is also a battered tin awning supported by tall iron poles sheltering the front sidewalk, on Broad Street. It would be an ideal place for an old-timers' bench. A father-and-son operation for the past twenty-two years, Hurlock's carries on in the tradition of W. C. Bardley and Son, the earlier father-and-son team that opened the store in 1899 and ran it for the next fifty years.

Brooks Parker, 75, bought the Bardley store in 1971 and now runs it with his son, Buddy, 50, who shares the Mr. Fixit duties with Joe Knoll, 77, who has answered questions at the store and advised people how to do things for nearly thirty years. "We have old photographs of the exterior dating to the early days

when the Bardleys ran it and the only change that I can see is our new plastic 'ServiStar' hardware sign," says Buddy.

The store has a very high ceiling of pressed tin with wooden-bladed ceiling fans circulating the gas heat or air conditioning. The shelves are eight feet high and are reached by wooden step ladders and a rolling ladder that travels along a guide pipe attached near the ceiling. Another throwback to the old days is a hand-powered freight elevator lowered by a system of ropes and an upstairs pulley wheel five feet in diameter. "An undertaker used this elevator to haul coffins that he stored on the second floor," says Buddy.

They also operate an outmoded charge-it system. "We know all our customers by their first names," he explains, "so if they come in and want to charge something until pay day on Friday, for example, we just make a note by the cash register."

A jot-'em-down hardware store with a jot-'em-down charge book in a jot-'em-down kind of town on the Upper Eastern Shore of Maryland.

Vince Jameson, Tobacco Farmer, Port Tobacco 〜

It is difficult to imagine the Port Tobacco of today as one of the busiest seaports in the New World, prominently located on all charts and maps during an era when tobacco was so important it was described as "our meat, drinke, cloathing and monies." For miles and miles around, wherever the land could be tilled, tobacco grew in profusion in Charles County and the rest of Southern Maryland, until "the sotte weed" overtook everything and became the largest agricultural crop in Maryland. Up until the early 1980s, it was a $57 million crop farmed on 27,000 Maryland acres, but in 1991 those numbers had fallen to $21 million and 8,600 acres.

As the hilly lowlands around Port Tobacco were cleared for farming, the soil runoff silted up Port Tobacco River and closed it to sea-going ships. Its commercial establishments today include only a marina, Murphy's General Store, a post office, and several tobacco farmers who will eventually be squeezed out by developers and the remaining farmers growing other crops.

The little village, colonized by English settlers as early as 1634, is one of the oldest continually inhabited communities in America. It thrived for the next century until the port became blocked. Next, the railroad bypassed the town and ran instead to LaPlata.

When the 1819 Charles County courthouse burned in 1892, the seat of government was relocated and Port Tobacco became a town of the past. Recently, being within commuting distance of Washington, it has been enjoying a resurgence.

"I'm afraid tobacco is a crop of the past," says Charles County developer and Port Tobacco farmer Charles Stuart, 56, of Rose Hill, a 336-acre former colonial tobacco plantation that he would like to keep partly in tobacco. "Just a few years ago we had some 40 acres in tobacco," he says. "Now, as the profit margin falls, we're down to 25 and slowly converting to vegetables, soybean, and wheat. The state is discouraging the growing of tobacco anyway."

But Vince Jameson, 59, and his brothers Bernard, 47, and Melvin, 57, and their cousin George Williams, 70, still farm small acreages of tobacco in Port Tobacco. The land they till, oddly enough, is probably part of the silt that filled up what used to be the river port some two hundred years ago. "We just mess with it because we've always messed with it, starting as kids," says Williams. "There are no jobs for us. What else you gonna do to help ends meet? We enjoy working with plants and the land, and if we can make a little profit selling it, all the better."

Vince Jameson, a cook retired from a Washington hospital, owns and operates the T and J Barbecue Stand near Indianhead. "Tobacco is a hobby for me and my brothers," he says. "It's in our blood. We had fourteen children in our family. We had chickens and hogs and we raised vegetables and tobacco. But tobacco is the only thing we still fool with." They look forward to working with the plant from the seed up, watching it grow; sticking, spearing, and hanging it up to be air-dried in a barn with open slats. They go to market in March, hoping to make a small profit on this Maryland tobacco that remains a favored ingredient in European cigarettes. But signs point to smoking restrictions in Europe, following the anti-smoking trend in the United States that has pushed tobacco into an irreversible decline.

"It's a plant I love to work with," says Vince. "You're out there in the hottest time of year and working with it in the coldest time of year. And you have to keep up with it, care for it." The seed is planted in a seed bed in March, where it germinates in April and is replanted in May. When the weed flowers in July or August, its "topping" is removed so the energy will be transferred to the top leaves. The harvesting (cutting) begins in early August and the leaves are hung to air-cure. By February the leaves are prepared for market in mid-March.

When the Jameson family stops "messing" with tobacco, probably before the turn of the century, that could well signal the end of tobacco as a crop in Port Tobacco. "None of our sons are interested in tobacco," says Vince, "so there's no one to carry on the tobacco tradition in Port Tobacco. You can say that for sure."

Baltimore's Last Tobacconist ⟶

A curious, all-male ritual is staged periodically in Baltimore City's last remaining tobacco shop, located in the center of the downtown financial district that was once also known as Tobacco Road because of its many cigar emporiums and cigar factories. Fader's Tobacconist, at 107 East Baltimore Street, a purveyor of fine cigars and pipe tobacco for more than a century, was hosting a cigar sampling, passing out free Macanudo and Partagas cigars for tasting. It was almost like the good old days, with the front door open, the ceiling fans rotating slowly, and about thirty smiling men (nearly all of them wearing suits) smoking and discussing the finer points of fine cigars.

A few women strolled in by accident to purchase cigarettes (a necessary evil sold at Fader's), but they quickly retreated from this smokey haze of fragrant afternoon delight. The men lit up, puffed, smoked, and stayed. They had to stay, because there are few warm public places left anymore to smoke a cigar in peace.

"I'm the third . . . and I'll be the last Fader to run the place," said Ira (Bill) Fader, 63. He took over the firm in 1959 upon the death of his father, also Ira, who had begun managing it in the late 1920s. Bill accepts his fate of being the city's last tobacconist in an anti-tobacco era when the smoking of anything is restricted, but most especially cigars.

Fader's has striven to maintain its ambiance, retaining many of the store's antique fixtures when it moved to its present location in 1973 from 210 East Baltimore Street. The veined gray marble bases support glass cases and wooden cabinets, and a kind of back bar with hand-turned pillars and carved facades is stocked with tobacco-related products. Beveled, leaded glass doors welcome cigar smokers into a captivating walk-in cigar humidor with a wooden ladder that rolls along iron pipe rails, allowing access to sealed cigar boxes stored on upper shelves.

Some of Fader's favorite artifacts survive, as well, although they aren't in operation anymore. The two bronze countertop busts of Victorian ladies once sported gas flames, piped through cigarettes in their mouths, and customers lit up from those bronze lips. But after a woman in a fur coat backed into the flame and singed the coat, the service was disconnected.

The ornate, crumbling Fader sign is composed of delicate wooden spindles

and dates to 1905. It was saved for the new location and hangs above the front door. Under it a plastic cigar store Indian stands guard.

Bill Fader is also the last in-house pipe repair man, but he handles only minor jobs. In a small basement workshop, he uses the tools of Fader's last master pipe craftsman, the late Josef (Hoffie) Hoffman, who retired in the early 1960s.

"Hoffie was a crusty old Austrian bachelor who lived in a rooming house and had some success playing the stock market," says Fader. "His workshop was plunked down right in our front window in the old shop. . . . He was a real attraction and he loved every minute of it.

"He always had a sidewalk audience as he labored diligently over his pipes while smoking Turkish cigarettes held in an amber cigarette holder. He was never happy after we moved him downstairs because he was creating so much dirt and dust in the store."

Fader's stock in trade is still premium, imported hand-rolled cigars, selling from $1 to $18 each. But Fader's also gained a degree of fame for its custom-mixed pipe tobacco blends, a specialty introduced by Fader's mother, Beulah. Thousands of index cards keep track of personal blends they mailed everywhere. Many of these cards are in the handwriting of Beulah and Ira Sr.

"This was a mom-and-pop business and it had many ups and downs," says Fader, whose grandfather, Abraham, founded the business in the late nineteenth century and also ran a cigar-making factory on nearby Water Street. "They were burned out in the Great Baltimore Fire of 1904, and their factory closed in the mid-1920s during the advent of machine-made cigars. Then came the Depression and they nearly lost everything."

During World War II there was a severe shortage of tobacco products because of rationing, and now the Fader establishment is struggling anew with a growing anti-tobacco sentiment, although it has five branches in the suburbs and the market in premium cigars is on the upswing.

To survive, Fader's has taken on a little bit of a gift shop look and sells products unrelated to tobacco, such as men's toiletries, beer steins, hats, ties, and walking sticks; but Fader's heart is still with cigars, pipes, and pipe tobacco.

A Fading Baltimore Tradition: Pigeon Racing ◠

Every Saturday, a gathering of traditionalists occurs inside an odd little brick building with a slanted tin roof on the corner of Fleet and Ann streets in East Baltimore's Fells Point. The Exchange Feed Store hosts the area's premier racing pigeon fanciers, who talk loudly and excitedly about their unique sport and the prized homing pigeons that feed their modest egos.

Decades ago, "pigeon men" pursued their obsessive hobby in many neighborhoods. Visiting a backyard or a rooftop loft was as easy as going across the street or around a corner. Hundreds of lofts and many pigeon racing groups and social clubs were around, along with neighborhood feed stores where the birds were bought, sold, and exchanged.

Today, there is one pigeon-feed store left in the city and there old-timers committed to the pigeon pastime gather. It's still a surprisingly busy place, especially on Saturdays, when men who love pedigreed pigeons arrive to look over the "tipplers" (high flyers) and "rollers" (tumbling flyers) cooped up in old cages lining two walls.

It is not a pretty place. Paint flakes dangle from the walls and high ceiling, and the creaky floor has been worn thin by legions of men walking through in workboots. An oil space heater warms a corner where the chatting of the men mingles with the cooing of the birds strutting about in their coops.

It's a fast-disappearing way of life, reports Ray Spoone, 75, of Brooklyn, a dean of the pigeon racers. "I've been coming here for fifty years. I can't remember when I didn't have pigeons, but youngsters aren't getting involved in the sport anymore. You know what's killing it? Prosperity!

"During the Depression of the 1930s," he continues, "we had no jobs, no money, no cars, and nowheres to go, so we stayed in the neighborhood. We had time on our hands and empty space in our backyards and on our rooftops. So we put that empty space to use. We got involved in the hobby of breeding, raising, training, and racing pigeons."

The atmosphere at the feed store of Joe and George Bowers (father and son) in the middle of the city is strangely rural. A happy feeling of smalltown camaraderie is evident as men sit around on fifty-pound feed sacks and exchange the latest pigeon news and gossip. Behind a worn counter, piled high with heavy sacks of feed, are wooden bins filled with even more feed.

Sad reminders that the hobby is disappearing are seen in the notices posted on a bulletin board—pigeon auctions staged at area clubs by aged men announcing that they are "leaving the sport." The handmade wooden "nesting fronts," with little doors that flip down to form landing perches, are on sale for $1 each, along with old utensils used in the sport.

Regulars at the Saturday morning bull sessions include Spoone, a member of the South Baltimore Social Pigeon Club in Curtis Bay; Jerry Krebner, 67, of Rosedale and the Monumental City Concourse Association in East Baltimore; and John Steyer, 64, of Hamilton and the Hamilton Homing Pigeon Club.

Dave Glorioso, 41, of Lansdowne, is a proud younger-generation pigeon flyer and also a Saturday morning regular. A man of independent means, he spends eighty and more hours a week tending to and flying his hundred thoroughbred pigeons. "I'm a sick, totally obsessed pigeon man when it comes to racing pigeons," he says excitedly. "I travel as far away as Atlanta to release my prize flyers in competitive events, and if they don't get shot out of the sky or killed by hawks they get home before I do. Funny thing about pigeons, but even if mortally wounded they will fly home to die. You got to admire these birds. I know I sure do."

Glorioso says youngsters may get interested in the hobby if their fathers pursue it, "but it doesn't last. When they get to be teenagers it's all peer groups, hanging out, cars, girls, and part-time jobs. There's too much for kids to do these days. Pigeons take up a lot of time, work, and money. Most of our wives, they don't like it none too much, but at least they know where we are and what we're doing."

Flying the trained birds is the lure of the sport. "As soon as my wife goes out somewhere," says one of the last of the Fells Point flyers, "I run up to my rooftop loft and let my birds out. I watch them fly around for twenty or thirty minutes and, to me, it's thrilling. It's kinda like I'm up there in the blue sky with them, you know what I mean?"

As for the city's street pigeons, that is a sore spot with the pigeon men. Please, they plead, don't get those flying rats confused with our pedigreed thoroughbreds. Says Glorioso, "Our birds won't even associate with that trash."

Merv Conn's once-famous accordion school is no longer in Washington, having been relocated to his home in Montgomery County after the D.C. riots of 1968 forced him out. Strangely, however, he maintains his empty school on Fourteenth Street, a presence in spirit, if not in service.

Sadly for him, accordions were already on their way out by the late 1950s, when Conn, 73, was hit by the onslaught of rock and roll. He adapted for survival by billing himself as the last "King of the Strolling Accordionists," and still earns a living by playing and teaching the accordion. He lists himself under ten different accordion-related categories in the Washington metropolitan area's yellow pages directory. It is a measure of the instrument's decline that the Greater Baltimore Yellow Pages does not even have a listing for accordions.

As "Mr. Accordion" in Washington and its Maryland suburbs, Conn taught hundreds to play, including the daughters of Richard Nixon. He staged massed accordion recitals and maintained large accordion bands and orchestras. He composed, arranged, published, and recorded accordion music and sold, collected, and repaired the instrument. He performed solos at the White House and played his Cordovox at the home baseball games of the Washington Senators during the 1960s.

At the front door of his house near downtown Silver Spring is a small sign: "Piano-Accordion Studio." But where his old school once had hundreds of students a week and employed five accordion teachers, Conn now has only a few students and one teacher—himself.

The accordion is a thing of the past, he acknowledges, although the instrument is still a key member of polka bands. "I call myself the area's only strolling accordion master of counterpoint; someone who plays four counter-melodies in complex rhythmic patterns," he says. As a master strolling accordionist, he entertains at social gatherings and actually strolls among the tables playing requests and "creating a mood. All the other old masters are dead or retired. I'm the only one still available for bookings."

The youngsters now play computerized accordions and are tethered to their sound systems, he explains. "They can't stroll. They have to stay anchored in one

place. Me? I can stroll, play on the move, and keep the party moving and alive! I'm not an entertainer isolated on a distant stage. I'm a party to the party!"

But although he often says "nothing ever stays the same," he cannot forget the past and the peak years of the accordion school in Washington. He makes weekly visits to his old school at 3509 Fourteenth St., N.W., where he rents out the top two floors. The sign reading "Merv Conn Music Company Accordion School" that he installed on the front porch railing in 1946 is still there. "Twenty of the best years of my life were spent at this school of mine," he says. "How can I forget it?"

Conn is not afraid of the neighborhood. "I don't have the heart to rent out that first floor," he says. "I still have the music stands and chairs set up for action, even though all that died twenty-five years ago. They tell me I should take the sign down, but I just can't do it! I just don't have the heart to do that!"

Death for the accordion became a wheezing finality with the arrival of the Beatles in the early 1960s. "The bass line of the Beatles replaced the oom-pah, oom-pah of Lawrence Welk," Conn explains, "and the kids put down their accordions and picked up electric guitars. The accordion never recovered."

Conn still plays an occasional job, but he plays for fun as well, at various social and fraternal functions, "just to keep the spirit of the instrument alive," he says. "It keeps me alive, too. The accordion has been my life. It's all I've ever known!"

Conn lives alone in a house filled with memorabilia, pianos, organs, and accordions and with accordion-related material stacked on the floor, on chairs and on tables. A recent widower, he picks up and plays his Giulietti in an act as natural as his ever-present smile.

Tapping his right foot, the dapper little maestro with a pencil-thin moustache and wavy white hair begins playing a medley of old favorites. He sings along in a soft tenor voice, strolling around his living room, willing to play requests for anyone who cares to listen.

"There is one song I prefer not to play," he says, "and that is the one song that has done so much to hurt and stereotype the accordion. I love it when people smile when I play, but I don't particularly like it when they laugh. Playing 'Lady of Spain' makes them laugh."

Oldtown's Old Toll Bridge ⌣

In Maryland travel guides, there are often mentions of the LaVale Tollgate House in Allegany County as the state's first (and only remaining) tollhouse on the old National Pike (now Route 40). The 1836 gatekeeper's house is now open as a quaint historic restoration, but a toll has not been collected there for many decades.

Not far away, however, there is a working tollgate house in Oldtown, Maryland, where tolls are still collected for crossing a one-lane wooden bridge over the Potomac River and into West Virginia. It is said to be the only privately owned interstate toll bridge in the nation, although there is no marker of any kind pointing out this distinction.

"Can't hardly call it neither a gate house neither 'cause the gates don't work—can't get 'em down, so they stays up," says "Miss Minnie" Piper, 62, who heads a family of tolltakers working there.

It is not such an old bridge, as one-lane, wooden-planked bridges go, having been built some fifty-six years ago by local businessman M. R. Carpenter to provide workers with a shortcut to get to work. The bridge supports are stout concrete pylons, approved by the Army Corps of Engineers. Its use is not as a quaint side step into history, but still as a functional shortcut over the Potomac between Cumberland and Paw Paw, West Virginia.

Driving over the Chesapeake Bay toll bridges is akin to traveling on a space ship compared with crossing the Oldtown toll bridge. The load limit on the 317-foot-long, "low water" span is 30,000 pounds, and it is limited to one motorized vehicle at a time, although hikers, cyclists, and horseback riders may pass two abreast.

Tolls are 50¢ each way for cars, 25¢ for motorcyclists and riders on horseback, and 20¢ for pedestrians and bicyclists. Trucks pay according to the number of axles.

Some people are surprised when they find a tollgate house here and Minnie Piper pokes her head through her brick gatehouse window and sticks out a tin collections cup fastened to the end of a long pole. "Hey! What's all this about?" some will ask. "I tell 'em this is about a privately owned bridge and if you don't want to pay just turn around and go back on the horse you came in on," she says.

Occasionally, the bridge crossing may provide a bit of an adventure, because flooding high water covers the roadway. "When this happens, we close up and go home," says Miss Minnie.

Some intrepid motorists will cautiously ford over the bridge anyway, just as people forded the river in horse-drawn buggies during low water in the old days before the bridge was built.

Less adventurous travelers are wary of using the bridge at all, for it is narrow and has very low guard rails. "Some won't even cross when there's hardly no water in the river," says Minnie, "but we haven't lost a car yet . . . far as I know."

The bridge is owned by Frances Walters, 72, of Oldtown, whose late husband, "Mutt" Walters, bought it about twenty years ago from its original builder. Reports filed with the Maryland Public Service Commission show that the number of crossings annually has dropped considerably over the years, to about 117,000 in the early 1990s.

Minnie Piper and daughters Phyllis Dennison, 39, and Grace Piper, 36, take turns collecting tolls from 6 a.m. to 10 p.m. and until 7 p.m. on weekends. If no one is there to collect a toll, there is no toll charge—simple as that. Roll on across.

They know many of their customers on a first name basis, but the rest are known only by license plate numbers. "We put down every number, friend or no friend, and if we get one who drives right on through without paying, why, we try to nab 'em on the way back," says Minnie.

"We don't have no 'pikes' to roll across the roadway to stop 'em like the olden days on the Pike, and we don't carry no shotguns or wear no uniforms and badges," she adds. "What you see is what you get."

The Lower Whitehaven Ferry 〜

Nearly all the rivers of Maryland are now crossed by bridges, but only one river is crossed by two free, cable-guided ferries. They span the Wicomico River, with only ten miles of water separating the upper (two-car) ferry and the lower Whitehaven (three-car) ferry.

Local historians claim the Whitehaven ferry—offering a pleasant shortcut over the river and through the marshes to Princess Anne—may provide the oldest, continuous year-around ferry service in America. The ferry service observed its three-hundredth anniversary in 1992.

The steel-hulled, 60-foot-long ferry at Whitehaven crosses the 1,000-foot-wide river in a few minutes on a dawn-to-dusk schedule, seven days a week. Service is interrupted only if the wind pipes above 35 knots or if the river is frozen.

The pleasant little village of historic Whitehaven, now a retirees' haven with a small marina, is on one side, where the ferry docks. Only marshland is along the shoreline on the other side.

James Farrington, 70, has been a pilot on the lower ferry off and on for more than twenty years. Born nearby, he remembers when a wooden ferry was pulled across by rope with passengers cheerfully joining in and singing old heave-ho chanties. In colonial days, they rowed and poled across.

"Today, some passengers won't even look at you or get out of their air-conditioned cars to enjoy the river breezes," says Farrington, although even grumpy strangers manage a smile when they ask the fare and the captain tells them there is none.

A gentle, good-humored man now retired, he spends most of his time crabbing, fishing, and farming. He runs the ferry as a fill-in on Wednesdays and other days as needed.

If the ferry is on the opposite shore, a sign instructs motorists to sound their horn to summon it. The waiting passengers then simply drive on in single-file, turn off their engines, and set emergency brakes. It doesn't take long for the ferry to cross, lower its landing grate, and discharge its three autos.

In the summer, farmer Farrington displays baskets of fresh fruit and vegeta-

bles: corn, tomatoes, peaches, watermelon, cantaloupes, and berries. He also offers souvenir postal cards of the ferry to benefit his church.

The ferry is now powered by a small diesel engine but used to have two outboard motors. "Because the cable keeps us on track, so to speak," says Farrington, "we never have to worry about being blown upstream in a strong broadside breeze . . . unless that cable snaps, and that has happened."

A boring life? Nowhere to go except back and forth to the same shores a hundred times on a weekend day in the summer? "You'd be surprised," he said, laughing. "You would be surprised what kind of not-so-boring things happen on this boring little ferry." He laughed again. Asked to elaborate, he replies, still smiling, "Don't know that I should." On further urging he begins, "Well, I could tell you about the beautiful young lady who used to drive across wearing only a pocketbook placed discreetly in her lap," he said. "Now, I tried not to look, mind you, but that's sort of difficult in these close quarters. I couldn't close my eyes because, after all, I had to watch where I was going. Don't think I ever told my wife about that lady."

Farrington also recalls motorists who drove up one ramp and clear off the other side and into the river. "They got out, but their car floated a little upriver in the current before sinking. This river is 30 feet deep in the center."

Passengers will occasionally jump off the ferry and swim to shore to beat their cars across. Once, a ten-wheeler boarded and the ferry sank in shallow water before it got a quarter of the way across. Pleasure boaters have bounced off the cable lines before the cables had completely submerged and passage was clear.

"I've been hit by workboats," Farrington added. "Sometimes I locked eyeball to eyeball with crabbers who were heading straight for me but their minds must have been someplace else. I tried to wave them off, but on they came. I've been barked at by junkyard dogs, shouted at by wild men furious over having to wait," he said. "But I've also had a lot of pleasant experiences, such as a wedding on board."

Passengers arrive on horseback, on foot, and on bicycles. Even stray dogs hop aboard for a dry ride across, but some will leap into the water upon reaching the other side and swim back.

"Sometimes people will drive to the end of the road not expecting to meet a ferry, and they'll turn around and head back the way they came when they see me coming," he adds. "Others ask me to drive their car on and off for them."

One regular patron, Joan Maloof, even penned and signed a poem, which Farrington has posted on his pilot house:

> Each morning . . . the ferry:
> The same steel deck,
> The same diesel drone.
> Sometimes the woman,
> With the harvest-colored hair,
> Shares my ride.
> But only the river
> Greets me differently
> Each morning . . .

Elevator Operators, Baltimore ⌣

Baltimore's classic downtown office buildings are being overwhelmed, overshadowed, and replaced by modern soaring glass boxes; impersonal and grand boxes, to be sure, but boxes nonetheless, with windows that don't open to welcome a fresh breeze or the sounds of the city. They are buildings with little personality and charm.

Even in the elegant, ornate towers, where handsome brass-fronted elevator doors open to transport passengers aloft, elevators are now cold and impersonal carriers, because the uniformed elevator operators have been replaced by cold and impersonal push-button automation.

Not all elevators, however, are without the human touch. Human beings can still be found at the controls of some freight elevators and in some old apartment buildings off limits to the general public. Not so at the Jefferson Building, a downtown office structure that survived the Great Baltimore Fire of 1904, at the northeast corner of Charles and Fayette streets. Sadly, the once elegant main lobby has been "modernized," but one is still reminded of the past grandeur of the place by a marble-fronted bank of three of the most magnificent brass-encrusted elevators in the downtown commercial district.

Operated by a trio of uniformed elderly black gentlemen wearing white cotton gloves, the elevators startle some visitors, who stare in wonder upon encountering something they thought had long disappeared. They watch as the "car switch" elevator operator steps on a shiny brass floor pedal to open the engraved, ornamental outer door and then pulls open a brightly polished brass cage door.

Stepping into a carpeted chamber of hand-rubbed curly maple, visitors are able to see their reflections in the highly polished, solid brass panels. "This is a blast from the past!" one surprised, youthful visitor observes. "I feel as if I'm in some kind of museum."

Ralph Cheatham, 63, a retired construction worker, smiles. "We get a lot of reaction like this," he says, pushing the old Otis control handle mounted on another handsome piece of engraved brass. Watching through the closed, caged door, one may count off the floor numbers passing by on the doors to other floors as the ascent begins. No flashing floor numbers on an electronic display board.

"Some older folks say, 'Oh, my, I hope this does not go too fast,'" says Cheatham, explaining that he can regulate the speed to slow, medium, or fast. He can zoom eleven floors to the top in as few as fifteen seconds, or creep up there in two and a half minutes.

"Most who board our elevators don't even call out the floor they want because we already know where they're going," he says. "We don't carry on a lot of conversation, but they know we're here and we can tell them who has come and gone, if they ask. And they do remember us at Christmas with little envelopes of cheer."

But why the white gloves? Is it just part of the uniform? Well, not exactly. They wear white gloves because William Walters, Jr., insists they wear them. He's the elevator man who polishes the brass every night, from top to bottom—every last ornate spoke and spindle and panel and geometric pattern. It takes hours, and it shows. "He does not like fingerprints on his brass," says Cheatham. "And, as a matter of fact, neither do we."

So if you're searching for a blast from the past, take a ride on a Jefferson Building elevator, with a real, live elevator operator—fast, slow, or medium. But don't touch the brass handrails. Fingerprints, you know.

The Sawmill of Robert Linkins, Rison ⁓

Most of us have no experience of a sawmill. We buy our wood pre-cut and stacked in climate-controlled "home improvement depots," although sometimes we may have reason to visit a lumber yard, where the actual sawing process may be observed. Insurance regulations, however, are barring outsiders from these potentially "dangerous," splinter-prone places where one is able to watch, hear, and smell wood being ripped.

The old-fashioned, one-man sawmill is clearly fading, with steam-powered operations almost gone in Maryland. Some Amish people, however, still drag whole logs to a woodman, who may work with steam more out of religious convictions than for practical or economic reasons. But Robert Linkins, 73, of Rison, is not a member of such a sect. A retired maker of gunpowder for the federal government, he is among the last of a dying breed of operators of one-man mills. He lives in an area of Greater Washington that is succumbing to suburbanization, and still operates his isolated mill in the woods because he loves working with logs.

"You wouldn't believe what people will pay in a store for something like this 8-foot-long, 1-by-12-inch board that I'm cutting," he says, feeding a walnut log by hand into a whirring circular blade that is almost 5 feet in diameter. "I'm talking $35. I can give 'em the same thing for $3."

A widower who lives alone, Linkins is a tall and youthful-looking outdoorsy fellow who is as much at home behind a bulldozer as he is behind a monster saw blade or his father's old blacksmith's anvil. But his mill, off Route 24 near Chicamuxen and Pisgah in Charles County, is one damn hard place to find. "Used to be that I'd tell people to turn at the big rock at the gravel road," he says. "Some people found me that way, but lotta them didn't, so I named my own road and put up a sign on a wood stake, right by that big old rock that's till there: 'Linkins Road,' I calls it, after me. You still got to be patient to find me here, but here is where I be."

The tin-roofed mill, open on all sides, is nestled in a rolling glade surrounded by pine trees. Powered by a three-cylinder diesel engine, the mill operation is primitive compared with what he calls "those push-button," electric-powered sawmills. "I use this here hand lever to engage a belt," he says, using that there hand lever to engage a belt. He moves the heavy logs about not with an automatic log turner, but with a kind of grappling hook.

"I don't waste anything here, like the push-button mill does," he adds. "Most people, they don't value nothin' no more. They cut down a cedar or walnut tree, saw it up and burn it for firewood. No thought of the valuable wood that they're burning. No thought at all. But carpenters who know their wood will bring me the whole log, knowing that I'll treat it right, cut it right, and give them pieces they can work with and still have some left over."

He bought the mill some forty years ago from Bob Scott in nearby Nanjemoy, took it apart, trucked it to Rison piece by piece, and reassembled it, using all the same nails and bolts. He replaced the old gas engine with diesel power. "During the winter, things slow down and it gets cold working out in the open sawmill where they ain't no heat," he says. "So I move my smaller jobs back into my house. I'm sort of a Mr. Fixitman around here and people always have cabinet doors for me to make and falling-down chairs that need repair. It keeps me busy in the winter, but I got my government pension and I do OK."

The mill is a one-man job not because Robert Linkins wants it that way. "You can't find nobody who is willing to learn this kind of work, so I guess one day when I quit doing this you'll probably see a house standing here where my sawmill stands."

Hippodrome Hatters, Baltimore ⌢

In Baltimore, once one of the hat-making capitals of the nation—awash in a sea of men's hats before blow-dry hairdos all but blew them away in the 1960s—the name Boulmetis survives. The shop's business comes mainly from middle-aged black men who still regard a hat as an indispensable accessory in dressing up.

"A hat can impart a definite sense of character, or just be used to cover a bald head," says Lou Boulmetis, 41, whose namesake grandfather learned the hat-cleaning business in Baltimore around 1914 after he jumped ship while a cabin boy on a Greek freighter. "A hatter can tell you what kind of hat to wear, and not to wear," Boulmetis the hatter declares. "Remember the first law of hats: Do not wear a hat that has more character than you." Movie posters of head-covered stars such as Humphrey Bogart, Harrison Ford, Clint Eastwood, Charlie Chaplin, John Wayne, and others appear to back up this old bromide.

Grandpop Lou began learning the trade at an East Baltimore hat shop—in a neighborhood of hat shops—where, as an apprentice, he was given room and board above the shop. Photographs of Baltimore crowds from the 1920s and 1930s illustrate exactly why there were hat shops all over town.

In 1918, while still a teenager, Grandpop Lou opened his own place, the St. Louis Hat shop, across the street from his former employer. Boulmetis's Hippodrome Hatters, at 15 North Eutaw Street, opened in 1930, the same year as the (now-closed) Hippodrome Theater. The latter, a once-majestic vaudeville house, booked major live entertainment (most of whom wore hats) along with first-run movies (featuring more hat wearers) watched by hat-wearing patrons.

"Red Skelton, Bob Hope, Frank Sinatra, Abbott and Costello, the Three Stooges . . . they all came to our shop to get their trousers cuffed by my Uncle Sam, a specialist in tailoring; their clothes cleaned and spotted by my father Tom, a dry cleaning specialist; and their hats blocked and rejuvenated by Grandpop Lou, the hat specialist," says Boulmetis. "We had shoeshine 'boys,' too. We still have the old brass footrests, but no shoeshines."

From the outside, the hatter's shop looks like a cut-rate store with ordinary hats and caps displayed on rows of shelves in a modernized front window. But

behind the front counter is a hat restoration operation that Lou's beloved "Papou," who died in 1984 at the age of 85, set up.

Surrounded by dozens of old head blocks of solid maple—stacked together on a worn marble counter near wooden, pancake-shaped hat brim flanges stored on shelves—Boulmetis flashes about in a world of steam that can turn his place into a 100-degree sweatshop with 100 percent humidity. "We [he and his wife, Judy] discourage this kind of work in the summer and we take off the last two weeks of August," he says.

He uses three sewing machines, all squeezed around one revolving chair so he can swing from one to the other as the job dictates. One (a Singer, of course) dates back to the late nineteenth century and served his grandfather well.

Boulmetis wears an undistinguished cap with no personality when he pounds the old steam irons and uses horsehair brushes to smooth the felt naps, although he can choose from a propeller beanie or a Dick Tracy fedora, as his mood and whim directs. He has a cabinet full of Grandpop's antique wooden hatters' artifacts, some of which look like mysterious torture devices.

"There are some who refuse to accept the fact their favorite hat is dead, even after it has been run over by a truck, moth-eaten, or held together with duct tape," he says. "But their wish is my command, and if I can save something they love, they will come back to me again and again. Besides, I enjoy doing it!"

Lou was formerly in restaurant operations. He used to watch his grandfather and father work on hats while waiting at the hat shop for his mother, who was shopping downtown. Boulmetis was fascinated by the rush of the creative work that actually restored something and provided a real service. "My father Tom [now retired] and I, we used to help out during the holidays when everyone rushed in to get their hats cleaned and reblocked. And when Grandpop died, I just took over and moved the operation next door to the dry cleaner's where Uncle Sam is still at work." Alas, there is no Boulmetis waiting in the wings to take over from Lou.

In the early 1960s, President John F. Kennedy's full head of hair inspired copycat JFK hair styling for men. Covering the forehead with hair nearly flattened the hat business because hats crush hairdos. Hats did not work with Afro hairdos, either. As for hats today, the story is caps. "Everybody wants a baseball-style cap with a special logo or message," Lou says. "A cap has got to make a statement. One of my favorites is 'I Know You're Lying Because Your Lips are Moving.'"

Aado Vaigro, Formstone Man, Baltimore ⁓

Formstone swept through Baltimore's working-class, row house neighborhoods in the 1950s and '60s like some sort of architectural plague. Covering up the city's classic brick fronts with a cement-like mortar, it was hand-sculpted and pastel-tinted to resemble quarried stone. It was a perfectly acceptable cover-up, because everyone on the block played "follow the leader."

Many of these identical houses were built with a less expensive brick that did not stand up well to moisture and weathering. Hence, the brick-red paint, slathered on year after year with mortar lines "striped in" with thin, straight white lines. It was, while it lasted, a labor-intensive effort that boldly outlined the bricks and made everything look clean and new again.

This look-alike aspect was important to the Eastern European immigrants and their children who sat together on the same sidewalks and hung their wash on clotheslines in adjoining cement-paved backyards separated by chain-link fences. They often labored at the same plants and factories, hung out at the same neighborhood "beer saloons," and shared the same work ethic, hobbies, and sports interests. They were also active members of the same Catholic parishes, and at the same political and pleasure clubs.

The women scrubbed their white marble steps daily. Families cooked and dined in kitchens in basements and seldom used their front "parlors," except for special occasions such as courting and funerals. Enthusiastically and almost competitively, they decorated their front windows with elaborate displays for every conceivable reason. They also fell under the spell of sculptured cement, a process which has since fallen into disfavor among urban restorationists.

Aado Vaigro, 66, is one of those early formstone workers responsible for changing entire city blocks. Born in Estonia, he came to Baltimore in 1950 when, he says, there was only one company doing this, the Formstone Company. It didn't take long to catch on like wildfire, and soon there were around twenty-five companies.

"We had crews doing different stages of the work and we'd dash from one house to another," says Vaigro. Soon, hundreds of houses were being covered with this stuff every year. "I figured this was a very popular home improvement and it looked like it was here to stay, so I stayed here and got into it and, in fact, I'm still in it, so I guess I made a good decision."

Vaigro, who lives in Glen Arm and works throughout the Baltimore area, is one of the last veterans of the artificial stone sculpturing era still working full time at the trade, often repairing and restoring the "stonework." He calls his mom-and-pop company Modern Stone, Incorporated—Hand-Sculptured Stone Stucco. His chief mixer and assistant, John W. Kelly, 66, started working for Vaigro thirty years ago, "and we have been fighting every day since," he says.

Ironically, however, Vaigro spends more time removing the fake stone than putting it up. "I pull down the sculptured mortar that I helped put up thirty and forty years ago and now cover it with artificial brick," he laughs. "I rarely do a whole house front with sculptured stone anymore," he said while preparing to work on a house on Wildwood Parkway in Baltimore. "I do stone archways around the front door, where the wood frames have rotted out."

His beat-up 1981 Chevy truck is fully loaded with three tons of material, equipment, scaffolding, and tools. "This truck takes a helluva beating," says Kelly, "but it keeps on running. We go real slow up hills, but coming down, watch out for us!"

Working behind the truck and near the curb, Kelly prepares the mix of cement and sand in a tub. Vaigro lays down a sticky black ground coat around the doorway, over a network of galvanized wire, and waits for it to set up. He then etches and scratches the compound while it's still wet so that it will hold the mortar cement that he smoothes on with a hand trowel.

He works fast and deftly, sculpturing the stone with his trowel and then spraying on a limestone and marble "glitter" mix. "No two stones are ever alike, in shape or in color," he says, nimbly walking along a plank set up between two stepladders. He puts on the finishing touch by lightly "striking out" the mortar seams to reveal black lines.

"In past winters, years back, we were so busy doing this work that we draped tents over the scaffolding and heat was provided," he explained. "There's not enough work around to do this anymore when it gets cold, so I just do other home improvement jobs."

The Wildwood Parkway job was done in one day and Vaigro and Kelly happily folded up their gear, cleaned up the area of droppings and dust, and departed. Vaigro could not resist a look back at his work before he left. "Pretty, huh?" he said.

Jefferson Awnings, Baltimore ⌣

Canvas porch awnings have been as much a seasonal accessory of Baltimore neighborhoods as the more permanent white marble steps. But in recent years, in some newer row house neighborhoods, front steps no longer reign as prime seating perches, having been overshadowed by porches under cooling awnings, which also provided privacy.

In time, entire blocks of porches were shaded by canvas awnings. In a Baltimore ritual, awnings were lowered in the morning and raised in the evening to a squealing, rope-and-pulley tune. But many canvas awnings have since disappeared because of the air conditioning and television that moved people inside. Some turned to permanent, low-maintenance awnings of aluminum and plastic that cannot be raised, lowered, or removed for winter storage.

In the more affluent communities, however, the classic awnings, now sometimes in synthetic cloth, are making a tasteful comeback—not only because they impart an elegant look but because of restrictive community covenants prohibiting the metal and plastic shades some regard as a bit tacky.

The L. E. Jefferson Awning Company has survived the ups and downs of the awning business since 1917, when Leonidas E. Jefferson left the downtown Stewart's department store to make his own draperies, slipcovers, curtains, and awnings in his first Waverly awning shop.

Jefferson's son and daughter are still at it, working out of a peculiar, rambling brick building that was once a veterinary hospital treating the wagon horses that delivered the goods to keep the city operating. Jefferson's is a difficult place to find, hidden away in a rundown residential neighborhood up an unnamed back alley in northeast Baltimore, in the rear of 1600 Federal Street. In fact, the Jeffersons often post a scout to guide visitors to their hideaway loft.

The interesting thing about this business, however, is not that it continues to make custom awnings but that it performs a personalized service strictly out of another era. The small firm operated by Lorenz Jefferson, 82, and his single sister, "Miss Virginia," 67, not only custom-cuts each porch, window, and patio awning, it also removes awnings every autumn for storage and installs them again every spring. "After we take them down at the home, we also examine them carefully for

any needed repairs," says Jefferson, a mild, low-keyed man with a warm grandfatherly way about him. "We look upon our customers as old friends and treat them and their awnings as such. They expect this attention."

In the rear of this former stable with a high ceiling, carefully rolled awnings are stored, along with their galvanized support pipes, for the long winter's nap. Row upon row of hundreds of long cardboard boxes rest like rolled up carpets in the cool and dry darkness suitable for awning storage. A pipe cutting machine is set up in a small workshop area nearby where Jefferson stores aluminum and galvanized pipe fittings. An inventor of a patented awning pulley, he started helping his father in the family business as a teenager.

The Jeffersons moved to the Oliver community forty-three years ago and tore out the horse stalls to make room for the awnings, which soar to the rafters. "We have five hundred very loyal customers," says Miss Virginia, who has run the office since 1946 and keeps track of everything through a personalized system of index cards, many of them decades old. "We haven't lost an awning yet," she says.

On the second floor, bolts of fabric are spread out over large cutting tables. As with any sewing room worth its name, a bank of tough old Singer machines stands ready to handle the tough material. "Years ago, we had four full-time seamstresses, because we used to do a lot of slipcovers, draperies, traverse curtains, and boat cushions," says Miss Virginia.

By November, the drafty old place has settled into a slumber and the pace visibly slows. In early spring, however, the storage loft begins to empty as Miss Virginia guides workmen who remove and deliver the correct awnings to the correct homes from their long, dark winter hibernation and reassemble them for another season in the sunshine.

"It's almost a kind of rebirth for us, as well as our customers, when we start hanging awnings again," says Jefferson. "I don't know, it's something we look forward to as much as those who happily greet the return of their awnings as a harbinger of spring."

But Jefferson is uncertain just how much longer he'll be able to carry on the business. "After all, I am in my eighties," he says. "There's no one in the family interested in taking it over. If my sister and I gave it up, I don't know what we'd do with our time." Well, they could just spend their retirement summers relaxing under the shade of their Jefferson awnings—Miss Virginia, sitting on her Jefferson awning–shaded front porch at the family homestead in Waverly, and brother Lorenz sitting on his Jefferson awning–shaded patio in Towson.

Buckel's General Store, Bittinger ⌒

Country stores in Maryland are in somewhat of a last-stand posture, and one you visit one year may not be open the next. Those most likely to survive have third and fourth generation owners living above the store, with a pair of EPA-approved gas pumps out front and a fourth class post office inside.

These stores require long hours and a sentimental devotion to duty and tradition. But even the surviving storekeepers admit their days of operation may be numbered, so visit them while you can because they are clearly fading from the smalltown landscape.

In some of these stores, one may even find a little backroom bar and a pool table. A few house small restaurant operations devoted to take-out dishes or to serving neighbors at several tables. Furnished with benches and chairs, they openly cater to regulars, who hang out on the front porches in the summer and play checkers and cards by a coal-burning stove during the winter.

A few stores seem to function partly as living museums, displaying country artifacts and selling some merchandise and tourist trinkets on the side to keep the old-time country store spirit alive. Most of these stores have lost their little post offices, one of which has been recreated by dressing up mannequins and propping them behind a cashier's cage.

There are still too many of these wonderful little places to even begin listing them here, but they are all worth a visit and are relatively easy to find if one can spare the time. Just hit the small roads through small towns. None of these stores are alike, unlike the generic supermarkets that are killing them off. Each country store has a patina, a personality, even an aroma all its own acquired through decades of the kinds of activities to which change comes slowly, if at all.

Buckel's Store, in Garrett County, Route 495 in Bittinger, is but one classic example of a successful general country store. If ever there were an earthquake here, Gary Buckel would not be found for hours, buried under thousands of cans stacked to the ceiling on 15-foot-high wooden shelves soaring overhead. Buckel, 46, feels just a tiny bit trapped here in a store he bought from his father, Joseph R. Buckel, who bought it from his father, O. C. Buckel, who built the place in 1913.

"The lifeline of a country store is the gas pump," says Buckel, "but EPA regulations are getting too restrictive to make it affordable to keep an underground gas tank, and who can say how long the Postal Service will maintain a post office here? Take those two away, and I wonder if anyone would stop here anymore. The sense of loyalty to the neighborhood shopkeeper goes by the boards when saving pennies is on the line."

The postmistress for Bittinger is Sharon A. Lowery, who maintains seventy-seven rent-free mail slots (not combination-lock boxes) by the entrance. She waits on customers from behind a cubicle all of six feet square that is sheathed in oak and brass. It may be the smallest post office in the state.

How long Buckel's Store will stay open, Buckel cannot say. But another generation is aleady helping out in the store where Gary and his two brothers began working well before they hit their teens. Gary's helpers are daughters Candy, 16, and Leslie, 15.

Buckel lives within two miles of the store, which is open Monday through Friday from 7:30 a.m. to 6 p.m. and until 4 p.m. on Saturdays. It used to be open until 9 p.m., but business fell off too much to keep those hours anymore.

Buckel's Store sells a little bit of everything, from lunch meats and pet food to hardware, fertilizer, bread, boots, washtubs, and workclothes. Sticky fly-catching strips hang from the wooden rafters in the summer, and a rare eight-day clock ticks away the hours from its high perch in a corner. "Everyone wants to buy that clock," he laughs, "but no one wants to buy this store."

He also follows the country store tradition of maintaining charge accounts, keeping track with an antique, folding McCaskey register that traps accounts securely in place with a mousetrap-like device that snaps shut over the paperwork. "Ever seen one of these things?" he asks.

A purist searching for the perfect country store could well pass by Buckel's, speeding to Grantsville or Oakland. He has updated (some would say defaced) the storefront with white aluminum siding and hung a plastic Coca-Cola sign over the front door, but the interior remains "unimproved." Heat is still provided by a coal stove, so don't be put off by the new front.

Stop in and buy something, mail a postal card to be postmarked "Bittinger," fill up your gas tank, and, if it's cold outside, sit a while by the Warm Morning stove and listen to the local deer hunters and farmers.

The Mickey Mouse Man of Annapolis ⁓

In the sometimes over-regulated Historic District of colonial Annapolis—the oldest part of the Maryland capital, where exterior architecture must conform to certain historic periods and standards—there lives a creative maverick who conforms to no one's standards and tastes but his own.

Cleo Apostol, 90, is a retired Annapolis restaurateur whose front porch offends some and pleases others. He displays, in great profusion, an eclectic collection of handmade lawn knick-knacks and assorted "found" things. He is especially fond of his dozens of Mickey Mouses, which have led to some calling him the Mickey Mouse Man.

Other front porches in the Historic District march in architectural lock-step, decoratively speaking. These disciples of "good taste" follow the less-is-more concept when dressing up seasonally for holidays such as Christmas (sprigs of holly and boughs of spruce), Thanksgiving (corn stalks and pumpkins), and Easter (baskets of spring flowers and ribbons).

Apostol's porch, however, is merry all year around and observes all the holidays of the Hallmark school of greeting cards. He updates his decor on St. Patrick's Day, Valentine's Day, Labor Day, May Day, Veterans Day, Memorial Day, Columbus Day, Mother's Day, Father's Day, Washington's and Lincoln's birthdays, and so on.

But the hundred or so whirling propellers, windmills, dinosaurs, chickens, ducks, Mickey and Minnie Mouses and other Disney cartoon characters remain on station throughout the year. With all those propellers and duck wings clattering furiously in the wind, it's a wonder that Apostol can still take summer naps on his funky front porch.

"I first put up some Mickey Mouse heads on sticks one Christmas about twenty-five years ago," he says. "I left them up a little too long, maybe, but when I started to take them down some of my neighbors complained. 'Hey, Cleo! Don't take that stuff down!' they said. 'Leave it up. It makes people smile.' So I left it up that year, and the year after that, and the year after that, and so on."

Those who do not appreciate the Mickey Mouse porch have come to accept it by now. At first, it was considered an eyesore by preservationists, who have been

known to get rattled over something as harmless as the installation of a plastic rose trellis in the Historic District.

But Cleo and Mary Apostol have lived in their home at 79 Franklin Street—just off historic Church Circle and right behind historic Reynolds Tavern—for almost fifty years, so it's a little late for others to mind their front porch.

Lately, Apostol put up a sign in the middle of his display, asking people not to steal his figurines. The sign reads, "Please Don't Take any of my Family Members. They Like it Here." But as long as he maintains his woodworking shop in the basement, where many crude animal forms are in various stages of completion, he has a toy replacement factory at hand that could keep his porch populated for years to come.

Mickey and Minnie Mouse figures, however, are hard to find. When Apostol sets off on his morning, noon, and afternoon walks around town, he is always on the lookout for discarded Mickeys and Minnies. He has friends and family members on the lookout, as well. Such orphaned toys are welcomed as "family members" by the Mickey Mouse Man of Annapolis and promised a good home in his whimsical happiness. As Cleo Apostol says, "They like it here."

A Personal Museum of Ephemera, Hudson's Corner ∽

The lonely Lawrence W. Burgess sits surrounded by hundreds of thousands of once-utilitarian objects used on the Delmarva Peninsula from the late nineteenth to the mid-twentieth centuries. Leaning patiently on a cane by an open barn door and with his orange tabby, "Mama Cat," by his side, he waits for the visitors who manage to find his unusual museum off the beaten track.

The 87-year-old "curator, director, collector, and chief" of the Americana Museum is held captive by his vivid remembrance of things past and an out-of-control collection that grew beyond his wildest nightmares. He is stubbornly determined to save these surviving pieces so that others may appreciate their mysteries.

"I'm getting old; older than a lot of the stuff I got here, see?" he explains in his soft and squeaky voice. "I want my collection to show the younger and future generations how the older generations lived, get it? Would you believe that some don't even know what a horse collar is! Or was?"

Articles of common usage in the home, workplace, and on the farm that once made dealing with everyday life easier are stashed all about him, displayed in seemingly endless aisles of overwhelming clutter. It's as if a division of the Smithsonian Institution's National Museum of American Life suddenly decided to lay out everything in its attic for a grand public inventory.

In Hudson's Corner, between Marion Station and Pocomoke City on the Lower Eastern Shore, the incredible House of Burgess, off Route 667, is identified only by a faded, barely legible sign reading, "The Americana Museum." Burgess also maintains a country store museum nearby in a converted chicken house in front of his home, to preserve his memories of country stores.

Burgess, who began informally assembling this monumental collection forty years ago, is usually at his museum by early afternoon. He sits on a wooden chair, near the entrance, where there is some light. The museum interior waits in the darkness beyond.

Outwardly, the structure, near his red brick home, still looks like the three-story broiler chicken hatchery that housed 42,000 chickens until 1974, when his collection took over the first two floors and displaced the chickens. It would take a whole day to examine everything, and it would be easier to recite some old Sears catalogues than to list all that's here.

Nothing is catalogued or insured, but the display is semi-organized, at least in the minds of Lawrence and Gladys Burgess, his 82-year-old-wife who shares his collecting mania that has, at last, ended. Ask, for example, to see some old hand-powered vacuum cleaners, washing machines, and butter churners (one a goat-powered treadmill rig), and they'll lead you straight to one small part of the vast accumulation.

Since a fall in 1992, the stooped Burgess no longer is able to negotiate the second floor stairway and aisles with ease, although he still delights in explaining the uses of the large and small contraptions all about him—if he can get to them through the clutter. "Some of this stuff is a mystery even to me," he says, tapping objects with his cane and reciting a litany during his personally conducted strolls of the unheated building.

What isn't crowded together on floor space leans against the walls, rests on long tables, or hangs from the rafters. Narrow aisles meander here and there, and one must be prepared to carefully duck under, step over, and inch around things. The larger items include tractors with iron and wooden wheels, horse-drawn wagons, surreys, sleighs, baggage carts, and even a restored black funeral hearse with a wooden coffin inside, visible through heavy glass viewing windows.

Housed in an adjoining hatchery and stored outside are even larger pieces, including massive farm machinery, monster tractors, fire engines, and older cars. Often, something's being old or obsolete was reason enough for Burgess to "rescue" it for posterity.

"It would be easier to list what is not here than what is here," says Burgess on his guided tours. He rattles off the names of things (many of which are labeled), spending only seconds on an item before moving on to another. Every now and then he'll giggle, asking, "Get it? Get it?"

The showroom floors are about 300 feet deep and 40 feet wide, and one can't help but marvel at what Lawrence and Gladys Burgess have assembled here, which leads to the inevitable question of what will happen to all this stuff? The fact that nothing is insured is quickly explained by Burgess: "We couldn't replace any of this if we lost it in a fire, so why insure it? Besides, we can't afford insurance.

"We're trying to give it all away to a responsible institution!" Burgess adds in a frantic tone, "I can't go on forever, you know! But there's one catch, see? The collection must be maintained as is, see, where is. Nothing can be sold and no paid admissions, see, although I do accept modest contributions to help toward the electric bill." The bare-bulb lighting, when switched on for visitors, is dim at best.

They have two married daughters, but the sons-in-law are not in a financial position to give up their jobs and take over a museum that produces no income and few visitors. "They are interested, but we accept the fact that they can't do it," says Burgess.

An electrical engineer by profession, Burgess was bitten by the collecting bug after he married Gladys Hudson in 1936 and moved to the Eastern Shore to help her parents run their Hudson's Corner General Store and chicken hatchery business. The Burgesses operated the store until 1974, while buying out four other country stores in the area in the 1950s and 1960s. They stored the growing collection on two floors above the store.

"This started the collecting ball rolling downhill," says Gladys. "We went to hundreds of auctions, at a time when things were still sensibly priced." Lawrence grumbles at "those damnable flea markets" and says he hasn't been to an auction for years and has stopped buying.

"I can't afford it anymore!" he says. "I'm a one-way man. I bought and I bought and I bought, but I never sold anything, see. If you don't sell the stuff you have, you can't get the money to buy the stuff you want. Get it? Get it? I'm a one-way man, see?"

Gerry Downs, Jr., Maryland's Last Caveman, Boonsboro ⌒

"Crystal Grottoes" billboards once lined the billboard-happy highways of Frederick and Washington counties in Western Maryland, tempting weary auto tourists trying to control backseatsful of bored, active children to "STOP AND VISIT!"

There was a running mileage countdown from billboard to billboard, along with pointing arrows: Only 70 miles to Crystal Grottoes! Only 65 miles to Crystal Grottoes! Only 60 miles to . . . And then, just outside Boonsboro, on Route 34, came the magic sign bringing relief to vacationing families mesmerized by this parade of billboards: "THIS IS IT! CRYSTAL GROTTOES CAVERNS!"

Well, Crystal Grottoes, the state's only commercial "show" cave, still has the "THIS IS IT!" sign at the entrance. But a highway beautification bill did away with all those billboards, so today one must keep a sharp lookout for the place.

This cavern differs greatly from its more-famous Virginia counterparts, the Luray and Skyline caverns with their Disney-like colored lights and paved walkways. "You want Disney World, go to those show biz places," says caveman Gerry E. Downs, Jr., 37, the third family member in charge of the cavern. The bearded Downs, a gruff and occasionally sarcastic bear of a chainsmoker with a ponytail, cannot bear to mention the names of "those phoney-baloney tourist traps," as he calls them.

"Our place is kept natural because how in the hell can you improve on something nature created over a couple hundred million years! I mean, look around, man! As long as I'm running things here I will never set up a caveburger stand or Fred Flintstone carnival rides and destroy this masterpiece of nature!"

Downs has a point. His cave, with some 800 linear feet of natural paths, is kept in a natural state with only 250 floodlights in strategic locations lighting up formations which look like frozen overflowing pancake batter and clay "icicles." Some of these eerie, other-worldly formations have names: Old Father Time, Egyptian Mummy, Old Sam the Turtle.

There are stalactites—dripping clay "candles" of lime hanging from the cave roof, formed by the evaporation of dripping water filled with lime seeping through the topsoil. And stalagmites built from the floor up, the result of eons of drippings from overhead. "This ain't exactly done overnight, man," says Downs.

A born promoter, who hypes his cave as "having more formations per square foot than any other cavern known to man," Downs grew up exploring these caverns. "This was my playground when I was a kid," he says. "It's all I ever thought about."

It's still the premier thing on his mind, because these caverns are how he supports his family and other relatives living nearby. He leases the caverns from his grandmother, Roxie Downs, whose husband, Ralph, developed the fantasy hole in the ground in the early 1920s after it was discovered by accident while blasting a limestone hill. It has been operated by family members ever since, but there were some lean years.

There continues to be something quaintly primitive, as far as tourist attractions go, about the two-story stone "cavern office" built into the side of a rocky outcropping alongside Route 34 and directly over the cavern entrance. A stream rushes by a gravel parking lot, "and about the only exciting thing happening here is when a tourist occasionally backs into the stream and we have to pull his car out with a tractor," says Downs, laughing and coughing while lighting up another cigarette.

Inside the one-room office is a showcase of calcite crystal trinkets, cushioned in little cardboard jewelry boxes, that cost from $1 to $5. "Kids love these souvenirs," he says, stoking a wood stove on a winter weekend when tourist traffic has dropped to the rate of a stalactite drip. "On a good summer day we can draw a thousand people here."

The tour lasts about forty minutes ($7 for adults and $3.50 for children under 12). It starts at what looks like a basement stairway that descends to the netherworld from right in the center of the office. Flashlights are passed out and the groups walk down a small flight of wooden steps and into the underground chamber.

A sump pump is rigged at the foot of the entrance and sometimes the party has to wait until a puddle is drained. The natural, flat path is smooth hard mud and the walls are clammy to the touch. Drips from high overhead often hit human targets below, so it's not a bad idea to wear a cap and rubber boots, although it isn't necessary—nothing is going to fall down.

Downs's patter is filled with little witticisms and wise cracks. He talks fast, but he knows what he's talking about. "The probability for more discovery is here and it excites me," he says. "One of these days I'm going to open up some chambers and pump them out with a hose," he continues. "It will cost a couple hundred thousand bucks, but it will be more efficient than buckets and shovels. Can you imagine the wonders we might discover? Who couldn't get excited about that, man? Besides, it would be a great promo, wouldn't it? I mean, it would bring tourists back who have already seen this place, right?"

The cave has been mapped by Downs and cavers, but the lure of what may be waiting beyond is a strong one, capturing his imagination. "I want to be the first human to lay eyes on what has taken a couple hundred million years to create!"

When he isn't a one-man band circulating brochures within a 300-mile radius, he is thinking of ways to promote the family legacy and draw in tourists. At times in the past he has hired teenagers to don a shabby caveman's Halloween costume, and sometimes he wears it himself and cavorts by the roadway to draw attention to the cave.

"I've put in years of hard work to keep this thing going," he says. "My family depends on me. Things do not run on their own in this world, man. I want to present a show cave worth the money, and I want to generate as much traffic as possible. It's a labor of love more than anything else, and it's the only way of life I've ever known."

The next time you see a caveman waving frantically at your passing car on Route 34 outside of Boonsboro, turn in and make a visit. After all, it's the only commercial cavern left in Maryland.

The Coal Man Cometh in Baltimore ⌒

Not long ago, coal trucks roaming the streets of Baltimore making home deliveries were a familiar wintertime sight, along with ice trucks servicing the same homes in summertime. The coming of electric refrigerators, however, made the ice man a thing of the past, and modernized home furnaces burning oil and natural gas have replaced most basement coal-fired furnaces.

Although the ice man no longer maketh home deliveries, at least one coal man in Baltimore still does. Clyde K. Adams, 72, claims he has the city's last independent coal business, operating under his ownership since 1946. "When I started in this business just after World War II, I bet there were about a hundred or more independents and full-sized coal companies in the city. Now there's just me still making home deliveries."

While he no longer drives a dump truck that tilts the load and propels coal down a chute leading into a basement, he still delivers the fossil fuel by the bagful to homes and businesses. Adams gets Pennsylvania coal delivered from Underkoffler Coal Service in Lykens. In the winter of 1993, he was paying $2,000 for a twenty-three ton load and, in turn, charging $5 for an eighty-pound bag of coal.

During the winters, Adams is usually busy in his Gold Street coal yard helping his son, Corey, 21, and some other men fill dozens of old, square canvas bags with hard anthracite coal. Using a large-faced shovel to dig into a coal pile in the rear of his rambling coal yard off Pennsylvania Avenue, Adams carefully keeps count of the eighty-pound bags as they are piled three deep on a beat-up truck.

Pointing to a little shack now serving as a storage shed, Adams reports that there had been a coal yard here long before he arrived. He also has a shedlike office on the first floor of a small two-story building with little nooks and crannies crammed with equipment and supplies related to his coal and tractor trailer business.

The yard has doubled in size, mainly to handle his long-distance trailer rigs and cabs. "These days, I haul as much freight as I do coal," he explains. "The coal business has fallen off and, besides, it only lasts four or five months. I got to have something else going, so I deliver freight with my long-distance tractor trailer."

His little office is heated by a large coal stove, which is also used to cook stews of turkey wings and rice and to boil water. A kind of workbench-table is filled with assorted tools, and a few battered chairs are scattered about on the cement floor. Adams keeps track of his deliveries at a high, wooden stand-up counter filled with scraps of paper.

In one adjoining room in the rear of his cavelike office is a large, roaring coal furnace with a blower fan. It heats the Greater Temple of Praise Apostolic Church located at the other end of the coal yard.

"We deliver throughout the metropolitan area," says Adams. "Most of our customers have small wood-burning coal stoves and fireplace inserts to cut down on the expense of heating."

As he completed paper work, Corey and two helpers opened the large yard gates. Adams immediately closed and locked the gates behind them as they left. This is a tough neighborhood and he is cautious.

The 1979 truck rumbled out of the Gold Street yard, turned left on Pennsylvania Avenue, and headed toward West Baltimore to make a delivery to one of the few remaining homes in the city still equipped with a central coal furnace. Adams says he has fewer than twenty-five customers in the city and metropolitan area who still heat their homes with these outdated furnaces.

The coal truck arrived at its destination and double-parked in the wrong lane, facing oncoming traffic, in front of 2525 West Baltimore Street, where Henry Bundy, 70, was waiting inside an open basement window. It was a scene totally out of the past, one common in the 1950s, before coal furnaces were converted into oil and natural gas. No one then would have bothered to look, but a stranger who had followed this crew was mesmerized.

Corey Adams carried thirteen heavy bags, one by one, from the truck to the open window and dumped them into a coal stall where Bundy was waiting with a rake. Beyond him was the coal furnace that has been heating this house for more than fifty years. "It gives me something to do," says Bundy, a retired army sergeant who has lived here for thirty-five years. "I like it. I stoke and bank the fire every night at eleven o'clock and feed it again at six the next morning. It ain't failed me yet."

Joseph Turner, the Button Man, Baltimore ⌣

A tall and narrow four-story brick building in the 100 block of West Saratoga Street in downtown Baltimore looks much as it did in 1920, when Joseph Tousant Turner, 92, began working there as an "all-around man." Still etched in gold leaf on the front window of Number 10 is "Simon Button and Plaiting Co. Est. 1864." But there is little button work and no plaiting (an old-fashioned word for pleating) going on anymore. Zippers and Velcro have cut into the button business. Button-holing was something of a tailoring specialty back when people made their own clothes.

"There were nine pretty young ladies busy working the button, button hole, and plaiting machines when I came here from Nanticoke on the Eastern Shore," says Turner. "My, oh my, but this place was noisy and busy then. No, no, no! Never occurred to me that one day I would be able to buy this place from the Simons. I had come to the city to get me a wife and a job, that's all. But no wife at this firm for me. They was all white, you see."

Turner, a bright and lively man with a wonderful sense of humour and a penchant for dressing like a bank president, was a mechanically-gifted farmboy who picked up the cranky ways of the cumbersome machinery by "studying" the outside repair men who kept it going. Today the brutish machinery, a ghostworks from another age, is still and covered with dust.

Bachelor Ben Simon and his spinster sister, Gertrude, lived above the shop and knew nothing about the machinery until Turner taught them, after he had learned by keen observation. The Simons inherited the business from their father, Tobias, who established it during the Civil War. "I figured if I learned how to repair the machinery, I could save the Simons money," he says. "After all, they were paying me all of $11 for a seventy-five-hour work week. I just wanted to give them their money's worth, that's all."

Up until the early 1990s, when he had a stroke, Turner arrived daily at his shop and immediately began sweeping the sidewalk—dressed in a suit, vest, tie, hat, and gloves. It was a workday ritual that went back to the Coolidge era. These days, however, his niece, Beatrice (Bea) Simmons (not Simon), takes over when they get a rare order for something like a few dozen white satin-covered buttons

for a handmade wedding dress. They have a million buttons, along with the machinery that can actually do this delicate work. It is a delight to watch them perform these obsolete chores on a ponderous, archaic machine in this era of disposable, ready-made dry goods, when clothing is simply store-bought and eventually discarded.

"What happened?" asks Turner, rhetorically. "Women started wearing slacks, that's what happened! Who could have predicted such a thing as women wearing slacks! They went to work during World War II, that's what happened! No time for dressing up in dresses with buttons and pleats. They had snaps and zippers. Got to hurry, man!"

In the front room the Simons handled cash sales from a wooden cash drawer where a concealed bicycle bell rang whenever a sale was registered. Some antique signs still dispatch warnings that were fully applicable a half-century ago: "WILL NOT BE RESPONSIBLE FOR MATERIAL SHADEING WHILE IN PROCESS OF PLAITING."

In 1952, after both Simons had died, Turner bought the building and the business. He sold it in 1990, but continued to check on things. "When I saw three people trying to sew one button hole, I knew it was time to return for good," he says. "We do a lot of repair work for people who botch up things. We charge 25¢ a button hole, that's all."

The floors are bare and worn, and dust is everywhere. There is no air conditioning. Bare light bulbs used to hang from the ceiling, dimly illuminating the workbenches, but fluorescent lights were added recently. Boxes and boxes of buttons fill the sagging shelves and will never be sewn onto anything here.

On what may have been his last visit upstairs to a room where women once steamed pleats in a high wooden tub, all the paper patterns are still stored—in case pleating ever comes back in fashion. "I ran up and down these stairs a million times, I bet," Turner says, walking up very slowly and catching his breath every few steps. "Anything for sale up here?" he was asked. "It's *all* for sale," he said, wistfully. "Know anyone who wants to get into the button and plaiting business?"

The Elliott Island Mother-of-Pearl Button Factory ⌣

It is probably accurate to say that there is only one mother-of-pearl button factory in Maryland. In fact, this may be the only mother-of-pearl button factory the state ever had or ever will have. But it has fallen on lean times, because the market for real pearl buttons has just about disappeared.

Once it was the only industry on Elliott Island, an isolated marshland on the Lower Eastern Shore that even the year-around residents (pop. 50) call "the end of the world." Making these buttons by hand were four members of the Martinek family (father, mother, son, and daughter), and as many as eight island women.

Chester Martinek, 76, and son Daniel, 50, are the only ones still at it, putting in just a few hours each day in a complicated factory rigged in an inventive way that would have delighted Charlie Chaplin or cartoonist/inventor Rube Goldberg.

"Nothing is the way it was," says Daniel, once a full-time waterman who crabbed and oystered in Fishing Bay until 1992, when crabbing and oystering declined precipitously. "Now I'm back in the button factory making buttons, although I have never really stopped," he adds, grinding away on a huge, imported oyster shell while puffing away on a corn-cob pipe. "But there is not much demand for them anymore because most buttons today are machine-made of plastic. They're cheaper, they last longer, and only an expert can tell the difference between our product and an imitation pearl button from Japan."

Chester Martinek began making pearl buttons from oyster shells at the age of 14, in Passaic, New Jersey, where his father ran a mink ranch. The family moved to the island in the late 1950s and re-established the button business there, where it is not exactly thriving today.

If it is difficult to find a genuine mother-of-pearl button made by hand anymore, it is absolutely impossible to find the button factory without a guide. There are no signs on the island except for the one pointing to a boat ramp. The best place to meet a guide is at the island's only gas pump, in front of "Miss Nora's" country store, the only business open year-round. Born here, Miss Nora, 91, is the oldest islander, and her store is a country classic, although it isn't nearly as old as she is.

Daniel is proud to show visitors around his little button factory that once employed a dozen people. It is a one-floor, weathered-shingled building located off a dirt road that is practically paved with pearl button rejects. Again, as elsewhere on the island, there is no sign to indicate what business goes on here.

Inside is even more of a puzzle. There is an array of complex, belt-driven machinery powered by small electric motors, belts running here and there to drive various mysterious functions. Tubs and barrels tumble and shake, washing the dainty, delicate products on their way to becoming buttons, which are individually sorted and graded.

The whole process starts with giant shells from Australia, stored in several large barrels outside. From these huge heavy shells, many of which measure a foot in diameter, button blanks are cut out at a lathe coated in white pearl dust. The blanks go through many stages before eventually winding up at a modern machine that cuts a button ridge and punches the traditional four holes in each. "This machine eliminated the eight island girls who used to do it all by hand, button by button, drilling every damn hole," Daniel says.

Buttons are still graded and sorted by hand, according to color and quality. It is an incredibly elaborate and time-consuming process. The Martineks have barrels of thousands of glistening, polished buttons waiting to be shipped, waiting for orders for buttons to hold together elaborate, custom-made wedding gowns and baptismal dresses.

Daniel is a happy-go-lucky sort of guy who "loves" making buttons. "I grew up doing this and I can't stop myself from turning them out, even if the orders are not exactly pouring in anymore," he says. "It gives me something to do at a time when there are few crabs and oysters around here."

He is trying to groom his twin sons, Chester Jr. and Howard, 31, to eventually take over the little button factory. "They are trying to tong for oysters on the Upper Choptank River in a workboat I built, the 'Southern Lady,' but who knows how long the oysters will last?"

He also loves building wooden workboats, "but who wants a wooden workboat anymore?" he asks. "And what kind of work will there be for those who have one built? At least my two sons and I will always have the button factory.

"One thing I can tell you for sure," he adds. "I ain't about to leave this island. All the young people are leaving, but I'd like for my sons to stay and that's where the button factory fits into my plans."

One more tidbit: Daniel Martinek is also chief of the island's little volunteer fire department that, in the recent past, had only one small fire to put out—at the home of the fire chief.

Tony, Little Italy's Italian Bread Baker, Baltimore ⌒

Baltimore's best Italian restaurants — most of which are crammed together in "Little Italy," a tight little neighborhood of old row houses — serve wonderful Italian bread, freshly baked with no additives or preservatives. Baskets of this bread are immediately wiped out at dining tables, but there always seems to be more where that came from; and much of where it comes from is the homey family bakery of Tony (Ozzie) Marinelli, 81, of Little Italy.

Tony, a bachelor, was only 2 years old when the Marinellis moved, in 1914, to their new home and business at 321 South Central Avenue. Married to the bakery business, he has been there ever since, working seven days a week managing his backyard ovens.

Neighborhood family bakeries are fast disappearing, especially those where the family lives above the shop. Tony's bakery remains his home. It is in a simple two-story row house next to a very noisy tack factory. A small tradesman's sign over his alleyway is weathered and worn, and a crude arrow at the side entrance points to the ovens at the end of a narrow passageway. Hungry pigeons perch on Tony's roof, waiting for crumbs.

"This is my life," says Tony. "It is what I know how to do and what I have always done, so why change? How can I change? How can I retire? To retire is to die. Poppy-Pop [his father, Gabriel] worked here until he was almost 90, and he lived to be 95. The bakery kept him alive, just as it keeps me alive."

Tony has no retail shop or sales counter. The bakery is in one small cinderblock room housing the rotating ovens, dough-mixing machine, sacks of flour, stacks of wooden bread trays, and a long table where the dough is rolled out, punched, and formed. Trays are filled with bread and rolls, hot and fresh from the oven, and filled brown delivery bags are gathered together tightly by the door.

Baked primarily for commercial use, the bread is also available to retail customers. The bakery traffic is hectic and frantic. Visitors ("I don't have no time for visitors!" says Tony), fascinated with these old-fashioned surroundings, ask a lot of questions, which Tony does not answer because of a hearing problem.

When there is no bread for sale, retail buyers are put on blunt notice when they find the heavy iron door, secured by a two-by-four crossbeam, blocking off

the alley. Sometimes people will bang away on this door for bread, but Tony can't hear them. Besides, he says, "We bake 1,000 loaves a day, that's enough." We could bake and sell 5,000 loaves a day if I expanded, but what for? I don't wanna be a millionaire. What would I spend it on? Where would I go? I ain't married. I ain't got children. I wanna stay here until I die. Poppy-Pop liked it here. I like it here."

Tony's six married sisters plead with him to retire, but he refuses to budge from the house where all "the girls" were born and raised. The home was a German bakery in the nineteenth century. The Marinellis turned the first floor into an Italian grocery but then converted it into living quarters when the family began growing.

The old living room, with worn, bare wooden floors, is now Tony's office and parlor and contains a makeshift assembly of overstuffed chairs covered with dust cloths, a beat-up desk, a 1990 wall calendar, and a working television sitting on top of a non-working television. The window shades are pulled down.

Tony's bedroom is the old family dining room, although there are empty rooms available upstairs. Hanging over the bed is a framed oval photograph of his mother and father as newly-weds. There is a spray of palms tucked behind the portrait. On a dressing table opposite are many statues of religious figures and framed photographs.

Why does he sleep here? "Because I got to be near the door! When my restaurants run out of bread, they call to come over and get more," he explains. "I used to deliver at any hour, but I got too old for that. Now I keep about twenty bags filled with bread by the front door, ready to hand it over. It's easier than walking up and down stairs."

Tony smokes a lot and always has a worried, harried look. A hearing aid sits on a nearby table, and he says "What?" a lot. He keeps his belt comfortably unbuckled, which forces him to grab his trousers when he stands up in a hurry. He has few teeth and is difficult to understand. He seems a bit gruff and grouchy, but he is a sweetheart.

With no Marinelli to take over, the bakery is staffed by a family of hard-working Thais. "All my sisters' children went to college," he says, throwing up his hands.

"I was the only son," he adds, "so I was expected to help Poppy-Pop as a child. But I loved it. I ain't complaining. I made deliveries with a horse and wagon and we all cried when we replaced our pet horse with a truck. I taught myself to drive a Model-T when I was 12 and knocked over a street lamp doing it."

Tony laughs heartily at these stories and lights another cigarette. He loves to talk about the old days, although few of his neighborhood buddies are around anymore to join in. His neighborhood has become dangerous, and Tony's house has been broken into many times. He has been mugged, robbed, and beaten up. "They even come over the rooftops, like on TV," he says. "They once stole my front storm door, even! But I won't leave. This is my home. This was the home of my father and mother, where all the Marinellis grew up. My work, my life is here. How can I leave it?"

The Last of the Home-Delivery Milkmen, Crofton ⌣

Before most mothers had cars and jobs and toddlers went to child care centers, there were milkmen who delivered to the home. They brought milk in glass bottles and wore company uniforms with their first names stitched over their shirt pockets.

Home delivery of milk and other dairy products began disappearing from the Maryland scene in the mid-1970s, and by the late 1980s had almost become a part of dairy history—except for Pete Danna, 68, of Crofton, who still has his green Green Spring Dairy jacket hanging in a closet. Semi-retired, Pete occasionally fills in for his milkman son, Scott, 25, who has taken over the Danna Dairy Products route in Anne Arundel County. Their route is commercial, but they still serve thirteen home-delivery customers, although they no longer accept new home business.

"We have been serving some home customers for twenty-five years, and we just can't give them up, even if there's no profit in it," says Pete. "One of our Severna Park regulars, in fact, gets just one gallon a week. It doesn't pay for us to deliver such a small amount. We do it out of loyalty and leave it up to them to cancel at any time."

Most of Scott Danna's home delivery customers live on Gibson Island. He has access to the homes and often delivers directly into the refrigerator. "Now that's what I call service!" Pete says, adding that some of his son's customers leave it up to him to keep track of the supply, too. "If we didn't have the accounts at the Gibson Island Club and the day school, we'd probably have to discontinue the home deliveries we have on the island."

Pete Danna joined Green Spring Dairy in 1960 and his route has always been Anne Arundel County. He became an independent in 1974, when Green Spring stopped home deliveries and turned over the county operation to him. The dairy still delivers to Danna's refrigerated truck, stationed at the dairy's old substation in Edgewater.

Scott, who began helping his father on the milk truck at the age of 10, took over in 1991. "I help him out when he wants to take some time off," says Pete.

They operate a white truck (emblazoned with "Grade A Dairy Products") that carries 230 plastic milk crates.

In the old days, Pete would drive to Green Spring Dairy in Baltimore and pick up his fully-loaded truck at 6 a.m. and return it in midafternoon. "It was six days a week," he says. "You had to be a good driver, a good salesman, and a bookkeeper, too. And you always had to be smiling." Pete wore the familiar green uniform and a tie, but not a hat. "I never did like hats," he says. "When I became an independent, I bought a navy blue uniform, but no hat. Scott makes his deliveries out of uniform."

Today it is a luxury to have a milkman, says Danna. "We charge $3.69 a gallon (early 1993), a dollar over the supermarket price. People who can afford it don't mind paying extra, but to couples struggling financially, with young children, the milkman was just another bill to pay that added up, so they cut us out. Who can blame them? It's just as easy to pick up milk on the way home."

Generations of Sugaring Time, Grantsville ⌣

It is a mysterious, almost magical sequence in nature; this time out of time, when fading winter gives serious hints of departing while spring waits somewhere beyond the horizon, preparing to lure anxious people outdoors again. It is a time when the maple sap begins flowing in the "sugarbush" (the maple groves) to nurture the trees and produce that timeless by-product called maple syrup.

Owen Stanton, 67, a Garrett County dairy farmer, remembers as a child helping his father and his grandfather tap their maple trees during "sugaring time." Now he works the same maple grove with his son, Joseph, 32, and his grandson, Brian, 11, the seventh generation of Stantons to work the family homestead near Grantsville.

Although the family ownership of the 425-acre farm has never changed since Grandfather Gus built the homestead in 1898, the method of sugaring has. "We stopped using horse teams about twenty years ago," says Stanton, "and in 1992 we just about ended hanging buckets on trees to catch the sap drippings."

Hanging pails under a sap spout tapped into a tree is a vanishing tradition, because it's easier if a gravity flow can be established from the trees to a storage tank set up in a hollow behind the sugarhouse. "It's a whole lot less work to lead plastic tubes directly from the trees to the storage tank, rather than constantly monitoring and emptying 1,900 buckets, bucket by bucket," he explains.

To preserve the old-fashioned ways, however, Stanton taps a few maples around the house and hangs a few buckets, "just for show," he says. "But maple trees are also dying off, and that's another problem. We lose about ten or fifteen a year to disease."

The magic mixture of nature goes something like this: Sunlight, carbon dioxide, and chlorophyll in the leaves team up to make the nourishing sugar that is stored within the tree in the form of watery sap, which begins stirring as springtime approaches. When this life-giving fluid starts flowing and "rising," it revives the tree for a new cycle of growth.

The first public sign that sugaring time has arrived is when steam begins pouring out between the open, wooden slats of weathered sugarhouses, where wood or coal fires boil the gathered sap in large vats. The sap should be boiled within a week of being tapped or it may spoil.

The Stantons put in long hours boiling, breathing the maple steam that's good for clearing sinuses. The boiled, crystal clear, almost tasteless sap flows into evaporator pans, where foam is skimmed off. It takes about forty-five gallons of sap to make a gallon of syrup. Sap turns to syrup at 218 degrees Fahrenheit. It takes on an amber color, and when the syrup "sheets" over it must be drained off. Hot syrup burns fast and can also be explosive.

The last step is pouring the syrup into a filtering tank before it is bottled. The process is finished in about six weeks, and by late April the gallon and quart jars of Stanton's Syrup are labeled and ready for sale at the farm for about $25 a gallon and $8 a quart.

"It's a way of life with us, but it's also a cash harvest, too," says Stanton. "I expect the Stantons will be sugaring as long as there are Stantons living here and working this farm and we have enough trees left to tap." Joseph is Owen Stanton's only son still on the farm, but grandson Brian pitches in, just the way his father helped *his* father. It is a continuing tradition of farming that goes back a long time with the Stantons, and Brian is there perhaps to continue that way of life.

Beaten Biscuits the Maryland Way, Rock Hall ⌒

The famed Maryland beaten biscuit (that's beaten, as in whacked with a club) has undergone a culinary change of near-metamorphic proportions, a change too awful to contemplate. It isn't being beaten! Modernists have taken to using hand-cranked meat grinders or, worse, electric machinery to "beat" the biscuit dough. Egads!

This mixing is not beating and simply will not do, say traditionalists Roby and Elma Cornelius, of Rock Hall, who insist on beating their biscuit dough with the kind of stout 33-inch, 32-ounce baseball bats used by sluggers.

"People have different ideas of what this product should taste like. My idea of a proper Maryland beaten biscuit is *not* a rock-colored doughball hard as a rock," says Elma, 75, who learned the art of beating biscuits from her mother, who learned it from *her* mother. Says Roby, "When I grew up on the Upper Eastern Shore hereabouts, all the children grew up beating biscuit dough with the blunt end of an axe. We always thought that was what made them taste so unique, but who knows?"

The Corneliuses turn out about fifteen dozen beaten biscuits a week, which sell out fast from their kitchen door at about $2 a dozen, mostly to their neighbors. "We aren't into commercial production and distribution or I suppose we, too, would have to put aside our bat and get a machine to 'beat' our dough," she says.

It's too bad that beaten biscuits are getting a bad rap, says Elma, who believes they should be golden brown (not pale eggshell) in color, crispy on the outside and soft (not hard) on the inside. They can be frozen, but they should be eaten hot out of the oven, she advises.

Roby Cornelius, 82, grew up beating the biscuit dough for his mother. A retired waterman, he later substituted a baseball bat for an axe for more leverage. He and his wife take turns swatting the dough for a total of thirty minutes on a maple butcher-block table. "I never figured out the mystery of beaten biscuits," he says, raising the bat and giving the dough a hefty series of whacks. "I don't know if it's beating air into the dough, or beating air out of the dough. You can hear the air blisters snapping when you do it, I know that. Here, Elma, it's your turn."

128

The bat is passed. The abused dough is flattened out. During about a half-hour of good swatting and pounding that rattles the kitchen cabinets, the dough blisters and cracks until it gets smooth.

There is something highly amusing in watching this peace-loving, elderly couple banging away with a baseball bat on a helpless mound of dough, but the results are wonderful and soothing. And, after all, it is a Maryland tradition they're carrying on.

They start with a 25-pound bag of unbleached flour and mix in Crisco (some use lard), salt, sugar, water, and double-acting baking power. The uncomplicated recipe is no secret and the Corneliuses are listed in the Rock Hall phone directory and open to sharing the mysteries of beaten biscuits.

"We can't explain how it works," says Roby, "but we can explain how to do it and *you* can judge the product." Golden crispy outside and soft on the inside. Let's hope the tradition of beaten biscuits is continued, although it is not something being taken up by younger folks. And let's keep the baseball bat operation separate from the meat grinder operation, even if we don't understand why it works the wonderful way it does.

Berger's Famous Chocolate Fudge Cookies, Baltimore ⌒

Family-owned and -operated bakeries in Baltimore neighborhoods still make cookies from scratch for the walk-in retail trade, but these bakeries are disappearing. Blame it on the chain supermarkets with bakery sections or even bakeries on the premises, snaring the one-stop, hasty shopper.

Also killing the familiar corner bakery is the proliferation of fast-food doughnut shops and convenience stores (more doughnuts). Those looking for sweets in a hurry don't take the time to search out the friendly old neighborhood bakeries—unless they want quality.

But as cookie monsters know, there are cookies and there are cookies. No Baltimore cookie, home-baked from scratch by an old family firm, has quite the national reputation as Berger's Chocolate Fudge Vanilla Wafer. True, it is sold in packages and not bagged, but it is still made and packaged by hand.

Berger's once tried automating its fudge-laying process to modernize a labor-intensive, fudge-slathering method using spatulas to smother each and every one of millions of these popular cookies. Ben DeBaufre, 64, who began making cookies for the Berger baking family fifty years ago, remembers the great experiment well, because it failed miserably. Baltimore's discriminating cookie fiends caught on immediately that they were being deprived of having an oozing, over-abundance of fudge to lick away before biting into the wafer. The cookies looked too much alike! The creative touch assuring consumers that no two Berger chocolate fudge cookies ever look exactly alike had been compromised. "They complained mightily," says DeBaufre, "so we scrapped that little cost-conscious measure."

Ben DeBaufre is slowly turning over the business to Charlie DeBaufre, Jr., 40, son of Ben's late brother, Charlie, who also worked at Berger's. The DeBaufre boys joined the Berger operation in the 1940s when it was on Bethel and Dallas streets in East Baltimore. They bought out the Berger name in 1963. "Now that was *really* an antique operation," says Ben. "The bakery was founded in 1835 and they still had stalls for horses there!"

In 1956, the bakery moved to slightly more "modern" quarters at 1821 Aiken Street in northeast Baltimore, on the corner of "DeBaufre Alley." The small, garage-like stucco building attached to a two-story row house is unmarked but easy to find: just follow your nose to the source of the aroma.

The making of this cookie is an all-male, all-hands-on operation. Trays are continually filled with crunchy vanilla wafers baked in revolving ovens. The icing begins with a solid fifty-pound block of bittersweet chocolate, custom-made from the secret Berger recipe. After being mixed with pure cane confectioner's sugar and melted margarine, the fudge is heated and continually mixed by hand in a large stainless steel container—which would be great for licking, although no one ever does.

When the process of turning out 18,000 to 20,000 cookies a day gears up, get outta the way! A remarkable sight in fast-forward, because it seems so antiquated, it goes something like this: Wafers are continually flipped by hand into a tub of melted, gooey fudge. Two helpers retrieve each individual wafer, splattering each with a slathering of fudge. No one does any measuring, and sometimes it looks as if they're overdoing it, but a Berger chocolate fudge cookie cannot be overdone.

"Once a lady asked how many calories were in one of these cookies," said Ben, piling on the sweet stuff. "I said, 'Lady, I don't have the foggiest idea. If you're worried about calories, just don't eat too many, OK?'"

As the fudge cookies fill up trays, they are moved to an adjoining packaging room on push carts where two women pack them in boxes by hand, about twelve cookies to a pound. The cookies sell in grocery stores for about $2.30 a pound and it is not unknown for cookie freaks to knock off a whole box at one time and pay for doing so later on.

Understandably, being around them so much, no one at the bakery eats these famous chocolate fudge cookies, which make up seventy percent of production; they also turn out cakes and other cookies.

"Maybe you won't believe this," says Charlie Jr., who has been working here for almost twenty-five years, "but we ship these cookies all over the country and especially to Florida, where retired Baltimoreans buy them. They tell us the cookies make them homesick."

While there is no retail sales counter at the bakery, Berger-hooked customers turn up at the side door, poke their heads inside, and buy whatever is coming out fresh from the ovens—which always includes fudge cookies.

Cramer's Five-and-Ten, North East ⌣

These days, what passes for a five-and-dime store is easy to spot, by the long, often red sign that covers the entire width of the building above twin entrances. It's a hard sign to miss, although the "5 & 10" designation has disappeared from most of those big, gold-lettered "F. W. Woolworth Co." signboards, just in case someone should get the wrong idea.

It was the beginning of a right idea when, in 1879, F. W. started his "Great 5¢ Store" in Utica, New York, even though it failed after three months and a string of other Woolworth store closures followed over the next five years. The idea finally caught on, however, and it remains with us today in a cleaned-up, modernized version, although a few old-style five-and-tens still survive here and there. Some even still have lunch counters.

Before Woolworth, dry goods were stored on shelves and hidden away in boxes under bare counters presided over by order clerks who were not salespeople in any sense of the word. Woolworth sold everything at one fixed price and literally dumped all his merchandise over large display counters for picking and touching. He instructed his sales girls to boldly say: "Look around and see what we are selling for five cents," rather than wait for customers to come to them and ask for something specific, as was usually the case.

In 1880 he expanded his line to include ten-cent items, and by 1890 he had added counter cash registers to speed up sales. Soon came mirrored walls, glass display shelves, and lunch counters. Others imitated the five-and-dime theme, although *dime* gave way to *dollar* and was eventually dropped altogether by most merchants.

But on some Main Streets in Maryland one may still encounter a five-and-ten in all its basic, bargain-basement glory, without any glitz whatsoever. One such independent classic is in Cecil County.

Cramer's Five-and-Ten, at 115 South Main Street in North East, has been around since the late 1920s and looks every bit the role, although it went through some updating about forty-four years ago. It still has the ponderous signboard that proclaims: "Cramer's 5 & 10."

Maybe its pristine state survived because it is not part of a chain that must fol-

low home office memos that order periodic upheavals of redecoration and modernization. There seems to be a bit of a stigma attached to the thrifty old five-and-ten moniker now.

Martha Nojunas, 72, has been working off and on at the family's five-and-ten for almost fifty-five years. "My parents, Albert and Jeanette Cramer, opened their first little store on Main Street in 1926," she says. "In the late 1920s they opened the five-and-ten here and it's been going ever since. I grew up with this store, and I still live up the street and walk to work."

The state used to be full of dime stores. Other than Woolworth's there were McCrory's, Murphy's, Ben Franklin, S. S. Kresge, W. T. Grant, S. H. Kress, Silver's, Schulte, Tommy Tucker, and the independents. But most merged or went out of business.

"Here in North East, there was just us and it's still that way," says Mrs. Nojunas. Her husband, Michael, 77, opens the store and the two of them manage to keep track of things in a huge shopping area that measures 30 by 135 feet. They snicker about one of their signs: "WARNING! Shoplifting is a crime. Don't get caught by the hidden cameras!" (as if there really were hidden cameras in this twilight zone).

The floors are bare wood and double planked, one of the improvements made after World War II, when they closed the adjoining twelve-room Hotel Cecil after the "war workers" went home and when the four-lane Route 40 opened and the dime store doubled in size.

"We do all right," says Mrs. Nojunas. Her brother, Philip Cramer, and his wife, Betty, help out in a pinch. They use two old-fashioned cash registers (one registers up to $4.99 and the other soars to $5.99) and a hand-cranked adding machine.

Almost everything is for sale in the store, even many of the antique fixtures, such as the twisted metal price tag stands that stand on top of merchandise. One might even find some "blackout blue" air raid window shades, along with original "penny post cards" with depictions of local landmarks in washed-out colors.

A pride and joy of the store is the penny candy counter, still maintained near the front entrance. Here they sell loose, unwrapped jelly candy such as spearmint leaves, orange slices, and "zippers," along with non pareils, sugar-coated Jordan almonds, marshmallow "squirrel nuts," chocolate drops, bon-bons, and other dime store candies from yesteryear.

They also have a seemingly endless supply of knick-knack souvenirs and have long kept a line of enameled pots and iron skillets. Asked to name her highest priced item, Mrs. Nojunas says she has an enameled clam steamer that goes for $35. To which husband Michael adds a correction: "Wrong!" he says. "The price is $34.98!"

But make them an offer on anything. One gets the feeling that prices are not carved in stone around here. And, best of all, this is a five-and-dime where you can still find items for a nickel and a dime; in fact, even a penny, as in penny candy.

There is no third generation of Cramer or Nojunas children waiting to take over, says Martha. "They all have their own things that they do," she explains, "and running Cramer's Five-and-Ten Cent Store is not one of them."

Bob Litzenberg, Decoy Carver, Elkton ~

All that is left of the golden age of waterfowl gunning in the Susquehanna Flats of the upper Chesapeake Bay are the decoys, tools, and hunting implements in museums and in the hands of private collectors. The game birds, for the most part, are gone from the Flats, except for the pet mallards that hang around for handouts at marinas and parks. Everyone has a reason for why ducks like the canvasbacks are gone from the Harford and Cecil county shorelines: pollution, overdevelopment, the disappearance of feed grasses, market gunning.

"I remember," says decoy carver Robert G. Litzenberg, Sr., 83, of Elkton, "when we had hundreds of thousands of canvasback prior to 1950. Now there's not a one returns to these parts anymore. It makes me sick. I'm always asked, 'Did they really darken the sky when they took off?' And how they did! They would darken the sky for an hour at daybreak. That's how long it took them just to get out of the river. They sounded like a freight train. Now, there is only silence."

Ironically, Litzenberg's memories of this vanished way of life have been preserved by the very decoys used to lure the birds into killing range. His unique, hand-chopped decoys are collectors' pieces, along with decoys by other carvers that sell from $200 to $200,000 and up.

He, himself, has become something of a museum piece, having been enshrined in a decoy carvers' hall of fame at the Havre de Grace Decoy Museum, overlooking the fabled Flats. A plastic lifesize likeness of the hatchet-faced Litzenberg stands in full work dress with hatchet in hand at a carving block inside a glass showcase displaying his decoys.

On April Fool's Day he sometimes dons those workclothes and switches places with the incredibly lifelike figure. "I'll freeze in place there with hatchet in hand," he says, "and when someone comes up real close to look into my eyes I'll give 'em a wink and scare the hell out of 'em."

Litzenberg says he is the last of the Upper Bay's decoy carvers to hand chop his blocks of aged white pine during the first stage of carving. He has a wonderful basement workshop with a low ceiling with floor beams used for hanging up all sorts of things. It has taken on a special personality over the decades, a charming

138

clutter of beautiful tools, unfinished duck heads and bodies, and coffee cans filled with artist's paint brushes.

"These days most carvers use duplicating lathes where they can turn out eighty ducks at one crack," he says. "It takes me about twenty minutes with my hatchet to do one, but I've always been happy with that method and it's too late to change things now. I'm not in it for the money. I give away most of my decoys to charity fund raisers."

He can't help but take a crack at the mass production that comes out of the duplicating machines: "I suppose they're OK to put on a mantelpiece."

His house is filled with his handmade pieces of furniture, and there are ducks on display in every room and on his back porch, which overlooks his now-empty dog pen and the backyard where he kept his English setters and pointers, Chance, Big Boy, Arnie, and Cody.

A retired painting contractor, Litzenberg gunned in the Elk Marsh and the Flats for rail birds and ducks as a teenager with his brother. "I bought forty unpainted canvasback decoys, forty blackheads and redheads for 40 and 50 cents each from Norris Pratt," he says. "Canvasback was delicious eating. We used to bag about six hundred a season."

He started making his first decoys more than a half-century ago, long before they were looked upon as "floating sculptures." They now feed a decoy collecting frenzy and are eagerly sought after by gunners and non-gunners alike. Today, every Bay museum has a decoy collection, and a major new decoy museum has opened in Salisbury—the Ward Museum of Wildfowl Art. The late Ward brothers, Lem and Steve, were Crisfield barbers whose shop was a living museum. Perhaps more than any other decoy carvers, the Wards heralded the popular shift from hunting decoys to decorative decoys.

Most of the great decoy carvers are dead or are no longer carving. The most prolific decoy maker (he developed a duplicating machine in the 1920s) was R. Madison Mitchell, 93, a Havre de Grace undertaker who died in 1993.

"The old-time carvers are just that—old-timers. We're all dying off," says Litzenberg, sitting on his back porch, surrounded by decoys valued as works of art.

Saddest of all for him, however, is the fact that his old bird dogs are gone, as well. He looks out back to his large, empty dog pen. "God, but I miss those dogs of mine," he says, getting teary-eyed. "But the gunning way of life is over for me," he adds. "Why have bird dogs if you can't take them out in the field? It would be unfair for them, as well as for me. But at least I can still go down in my workshop and carve decoys."

The Oyster Packing House, Mt. Vernon ⌒

A childhood highlight of the rural way of life in Southern Maryland for State Senator Bernie Fowler occurred when the winter oyster fleet came into port from the Patuxent River, "forty or sixty boats, all jockeying for position to unload in the sunset," he recalled. "There were 135 shuckers at Warren Denton's oyster house, blacks, and they would sing, sing more as they got tired, solid harmony. . . . You can't know how enriching that was," Fowler told Chesapeake Bay writer Tom Horton.

Times have changed on Broome's Island at Calvert County's last oyster packing house, established in 1923. Warren Denton is dead, as are most of the Patuxent's oysters. In the winter of 1992–93 not one oyster boat unloaded at Denton's Packing House, "not one bushel," says Norman Dorrell, who bought the business in 1984.

Oysters are now trucked to this packing house from Louisiana, Mississippi, Alabama, "and from anywhere else we can get 'em," says Dorrell. The shuckers number about twenty-five, and most are at retirement age. As for the old Gospel tunes, he says that, too, is a relic of the past: "They're hurtin' too bad financially to want to sing about anything."

Maryland's fabled oyster industry, which peaked at 15 million bushels in 1984–85, may finally be near an end. The harvest had dropped to 1.5 million bushels in 1986 and plunged to under 150,000 bushels in 1992–93. It could be the point of no return, although some experts believe the oyster could make another of its mysterious comebacks.

William Hopkins (Hop) Fisher, 80, operates one of the last of the old-fashioned oyster packing houses in Maryland and the very last on the Wicomico River. The white packing house with the tin roof at Webster's Cove Harbor in Mt. Vernon, on the Lower Eastern Shore, still uses potbellied coal stoves as the preferred way of heating. And opened oyster shells are still dropped through a "drop hole" in a cement work table at each shucking station, rather than being carried out of the building on a conveyor belt to a single high pile of oyster shells outside.

Oyster boats no longer unload at Webster's Cove, because there are not enough live oysters in nearby Monie Bay to justify working the beds. "It's a dying way of life down here unless nature brings the oyster back," says Fisher, a native of Mt. Vernon. "It's as bad a season (1992–93) as I can remember, and that's going back a long time. Oysters don't come to the plant like they used to. We have to go to them, and that means trying to find them, if you can. It's rough."

Fisher employs fifteen to twenty shuckers. Wearing long rubber aprons, rubber gloves and boots, they stand on low wooden pallets to keep off the cold, wet cement floor. Some used to shuck standing inside cutaway barrels, or in three-sided wooden stalls for warmth. Many plants have been modernized with forced hot air heat and stainless steel work stations.

The method of opening an oyster, however, has changed little over the years. The shucker stands the shell on edge and gives it a sharp whack with a small metal club. The lip of the tightly closed shell is then opened with an oyster knife and the meat removed, surgically and swiftly, with a swipe of the dull blade and plopped into a gallon tin. Shuckers are paid by the gallon.

"Dependable oyster shuckers are harder and harder to find, because this is seasonal work and people want full-time jobs," says Fisher. "If we shuck 100 gallons a day, I'm satisfied. We used to do 300."

Upriver, and visible from Fisher's Mt. Vernon Packing Company, is what was once Fisher's Bivalve Packing Company. Now closed, the isolated oyster house at the dead-end of a gravel road has an abandoned, ghostly look to it reminiscent of old steamboat landing wharves fallen into ruin. "Someone came in and 'borrowed' my stainless steel tanks and equipment," says Fisher sarcastically. He has rented out the place in past summers for a softshell crab-shedding operation.

Fisher began operating his last packing house at Webster's Cove about forty-four years ago, although it was established there earlier. A Fisher and Hopkins family tradition could be coming to an end here, he is sad to admit: "My father, grandfather, and great-grandfather were watermen. My family came to Mt. Vernon in the early 1700s, but I may be the last of them to carry on this way of life. My son [Charles, 52] drives a school bus. I'd give the business to him tomorrow morning if he wanted it."

The possibility of a townhouse development with a fancy marina and restaurant replacing his Mt. Vernon Packing House seems remote to him, given the financial climate of the early 1990s, but who would ever have imagined townhouses at the nearby watermen's haven of Wenona, on isolated Deal Island, where most of the famed Tangier Sound oysters are also dead? Asked how "Ye Olde Webster's Cove Pointe in Mt. Vernon's" sounds, Fisher looks around and shakes his head at his empty pier. "I'd rather see the oysters come back," he says.

The Messick Boys, Tongshaft Makers, Bivalve ⌁

Over the years, oyster tongshaft makers Cornelius and Wilbur Messick, of Bivalve, have had increasing difficulty finding supplies of virgin longleaf yellow heart pine with which to make the shafts most handtongers use to harvest river oysters. But during the calamitous winter oystering season of 1992–93, they were in the curious position of having a plentiful supply of wood used to make the cumbersome tool. The problem was with the Bay's oyster supply, which seems to be approaching a state of collapse. "If there are no oysters, there's no need to build oyster tongshafts to catch them; simple as that," says Cornelius ("Corny"), 66, who is also the local undertaker.

Corny and Wilbur, 63, formerly the town postmaster, have carried on the family tradition of tongmaking in this Lower Eastern Shore town on the Nanticoke River. And they may well be the last of the Messicks to follow this sideline, because the next generation, while taking up the family undertaking business, is not into tongshafts.

"It's something me and my brother have done since we were children," says Corny. "It gets to be part of your life. There are other undertakers, but there aren't any tongshaft makers left who do this work on a large scale like us."

The two-man tongshaft business operates in a two-story barn just around the corner from the family funeral home, where Corny lives. A huge pile of sawn timber, luckily acquired in 1991 in Georgia, takes up most of the first floor, where all the sawing, shaping, sanding, clamping, and gluing goes on. About sixteen operations are involved in making a pair of tongshafts, and each pair has "Messick Bros." burned into the wood.

"We got all this wood when we had the chance," explains Corny. "We had to buy 118 trees that had to be sawn and trucked here. There will be a lot of waste, but we couldn't be selective. We had to take what we could get. Some will be too soft, or too heavy, or the grain won't be just right. This is very special, slow growing wood. It has a real dense grain; is strong and flexible, and it must be available in lengths up to 20 feet."

Most tongshafts are in the 16- to 18-foot range and sell for $7 a foot. A 34-footer is $442, although they have made shafts as long as 36 feet. Tongers need

more than one pair, according to the depth of the waters they're working. The scissor-like apparatus pivots on a low pin as the tonger, standing on the edge of his boat, works the tongshafts. The two opposing iron baskets ("heads") attached to the end of the shafts clamp onto the oysters in their "bed" on the bottom. It is back-breaking work, and most tongers now use a hydraulic lift to bring the load up to deck level, where the oysters are deposited.

The iron, rakelike heads are made by welders such as Robert Condon, a Cambridge welder and hand tonger who gave up oystering in the Choptank River early in the 1993 season because the harvest was so poor. "You can't make a living when you can only get two bushels at $25 a bushel, and I can't make a living making heads when there are no oysters to fill those heads," he says, "so I got a job in a sheet metal shop."

Corny has seen the oyster cycle go up and down before and he's optimistic about the eventual replenishment of the stock. "I can't imagine oysters are finished in the Chesapeake Bay," he says. "There will always be someone out there hand tonging, I think, even if there are no more dredgers or patent tongers [with mechanical rigs] working out in the Bay."

Asked if tongs could be made for the tourist trade as souvenirs of a vanished industry, he answers: "That's too sad to even think about right now, but it's not a bad idea." A daughter is already in the sign-making business (Signs by Andrea) in Salisbury. One can even envision a new, old-timey sign: "Souvenir Tongshafts by the Messick Brothers, the Last of the Tongshaft Makers."

The Disappearing Skipjack, Tilghman and Deal Islands ~

The endangered oyster-dredging skipjack, that romantic symbol of the Chesapeake Bay, may be reaching a turning point in its long and colorful history. If the Bay's oyster production, which has reached historic lows, gets much worse, the last fleet that harvests seafood under sail in this country could well furl its sails.

Without oysters to harvest, this sailing vessel loses its reason for existence. Dredging under power is allowed only on Mondays and Tuesdays, but because there are so few harvestable oysters, many skipjack captains are not even bothering to dredge, under sail, the rest of the week.

"That's what happened during the winter of '93," says skipjack captain Wadey Murphy, 52, of Tilghman Island. "I really enjoy sailing the 'Rebecca T. Ruark,' so I dredged under sail whenever I could. But the other skipjack captains mostly power-dredged, got what they could, and went home."

A third generation "drudger," Murphy has the oldest (1886) working skipjack in the diminishing fleet, but it is also one of the fastest and most able. He overhauled her in the mid-1980s, at a cost of $80,000 ($60,000 more than the estimate). "If there are no oysters to harvest, what's the point of keeping an old boat going and beating her up to dredge for oysters that ain't there?" he asks.

In order to keep his workboat alive, Murphy is considering using her as a tourist passenger boat, he says. "I have to be a U.S. Coast Guard–certified captain with a license, and the boat has to be certified so that I can carry six passengers for day-sailing."

"If there are oysters, I'll oyster," he adds. "But if the oysters are all dead, Rebecca's gonna end up dead, too, if she stays a drudge boat. I ain't no yachtsman, and she ain't no yacht."

Murphy believes the oysters may be gone for good, "unless the good Lord does something. Same thing happened with disease in Delaware Bay in the 1950s. Now there's nothing in Delaware Bay. It's here now, mark my word." The 1992–93 harvest was under 150,000 bushels, compared to 1.5 million bushels harvested ten years ago. The dredging fleet, accounting for less than 4 percent of the oyster harvest, numbers under twenty-five and a few more drop out every year.

During the disastrous 1992–93 season, many skipjacks went dredging north of the Bay bridges for the first time, because most of the disease-stricken oysters south of the bridges were dead. The fleet operated mostly out of Rock Hall and Tolchester on the Bay, and Deep Creek in the Magothy River.

Practically the entire Art Daniels family, of Deal Island, worked out of Rock Hall. The Daniels fleet included a patent tonger workboat, Captain Art's "City of Crisfield," and the chartered "Maimie Mister," the only working two-masted dredge boat left in the Bay.

Also mostly gone from the Chesapeake, along with the working two-masters, usually called bugeyes, are the beamy old wooden "buy boats," which transported oysters from dredger to wholesaler. Now, most dredge boats unload directly at the dock and onto waiting trucks, using conveyor belts.

"Can't make a living and keep a boat and crew going on 25 bushels a day at $24 a bushel," says Daniels, 71, who has owned the "Crisfield" for forty years. "Can't do it, captain, no matter how good you think you are. There just aren't nary enough oysters out there to do it, is all."

Oysters were once the king of seafood harvests in Baltimore. In 1884, this "Queen City of the Patapsco Drainage Basin" packed more oysters than any other city in the world; forty-five plants employed 7,000 people and tens of thousands more worked in support industries. Not one plant remains today.

But old maritime ways die hard on the Chesapeake Bay. "Passenger steamboats and commercial sailing craft plied these waters long after they had been displaced elsewhere," wrote Bay historian Robert H. Burgess. Before change set in, notes Burgess, people traveled by country roads and along the Bay's many waterways, contributing to the use of steam and sail where they would have been outmoded if the area had been made more accessible earlier.

The age of working sail hangs on, barely, in what is left of the Bay's graceful wooden vessels with the long, clipper bowsprits and raked pine masts. "It is becoming impossible for them to continue being living museum pieces [and] marvelous anachronisms," says Bay writer Tom Horton.

By all that's reasonable, skipjacks belong in maritime museums, and some, indeed, have retired to those safe harbors. Most, however, have suffered the ignoble fate of being stripped and towed up narrow creeks, beached, and abandoned. A few are being used as tourist and educational passenger boats, and a Baltimore organization called Save Our Skipjacks has, indeed, saved at least one skipjack— the restored "Caleb W. Jones," which is dredging again. Two other skipjacks await their turns in the rebuilding shed on the city's Fells Point waterfront.

The old question was, How long will this fleet of oyster-dredging skipjacks last? Ironically, it now appears they could outlast the oysters.

Francis Goddard, Wooden Workboat Builder, Piney Point ⁓

Francis Goddard's fleet of Goddard-built and designed wooden workboats is for sale, but there doesn't seem to be much demand anymore for the likes of a 50-foot oyster-dredging skipjack ("Connie Francis," 1984) or a 64-foot oyster "buy boat" ("Poppa Francis," 1989). "Who would have ever believed that in this whole lower Chesapeake Bay there'd be no use for such boats anymore?" asks waterman Goddard, 62, of Piney Point, on the Potomac River. "But that's a fact. The oysters are gone; can't drudge for 'em with a drudge boat or buy 'em with a buy boat one."

An expert builder of wooden boats, known even to marine curators at the Smithsonian Institution, Goddard wonders if the 47-foot boat ("Miss Jennifer") that he built in 1992 for John Cameron, a seafood dealer in Piney Point, could be his last one.

Almost no builders of quality wooden workboats remain in lower Southern Maryland, and none along the shores of St. Mary's County. "Neither a soul I know of who's active in it nowadays," he says. "At one time there were maybe five or six doing it down here."

When Goddard isn't dredging for oysters, which he does less and less, he occasionally takes on a boat-building contract. He works alone, although his son, Wayne, 34, sometimes builds his own wooden pleasure boats. "Lord knows, I tried to discourage him from taking it up," he says. Goddard has no idea of how many boats he has built but he does have an idea of how much money he made on them. "Damn little, I can tell you that," he says. "It's work that is, how do they say it? Labor intense?"

A thin, rangy man with a lyrical Southern Maryland way of speaking, he lays down no plans or blueprints but works from informal sketches and then by "rack of eye." He cross-planks the bottoms of his boats because it's cheaper to replace a plank that way. And he does not cotton-caulk his seams. The glued planks fit together so perfectly that, once they swell a bit in the water, they're even tighter.

John Cameron, who lives in Fort Washington, has three Goddard-built boats: a 44-foot charter fishing "head" boat ("Susan Gail," 1981); a 38-foot workboat ("Bushwacker," 1974) used for crabbing by his son John Jr.; and "Miss Jeanette," used for crabbing and hauling fish for crab bait.

"I suppose that shows what I think of Goddard boats, having three of them," he says. "Except for the older wooden boats out there, almost everyone has fiberglass vessels today," he continues. "I don't think they can take the pounding when pushed as hard as workboats. Goddard boats absorb the pounding and the strain. They hold up better, and the boat will lay with you while you're working the crabpots and not blow off in the wind like a plastic boat. But the most amazing thing about them is they don't leak. It's uncanny."

Goddard carefully fastens and reinforces his boats so they will not "work," that is, loosen, and will hold together. "I don't work alone because I like it, although maybe I do a little bit," he says. "Besides, you can't find anyone who wants to help or learn how to do it. And when I work, I don't talk, so don't visit with me when I'm building a boat, because I won't talk with you."

The boatbuilding is done out in a temporary shed behind his house rigged with a roof of clear plastic sheeting to keep the rain out and let the light in. The material that goes into a boat varies according to what the contractor wants to spend. "I use a lot of country spruce, usually for the bottom," he says. "And white oak, for framing, and pine and juniper [white cedar]."

Goddard was born in Piney Point, as were his father and grandfather, who were watermen and farmers. "My father couldn't drive a nail," he says, "so I guess I learned from Grandpop, who was a pretty good carpenter. I built my first boat, a skiff, when I was about 11 years old."

He says he always builds his boats "in bed, before I fall asleep. I see it before me and plan it all in my head. It helps me get to sleep, too." He built his current skipjack from a miniature model; the other way around for most builders, who may start with half-hull models. "That model of the 'Connie Francis,' on a scale of one inch to the foot, is unrigged and on view at the Calvert Maritime Museum in Solomons. They tell me that because the boat was based on the full model, the model has become valuable. I don't know."

Goddard is unsure of what the future holds in the way of oystering, crabbing, or boatbuilding. "I know one thing, though," he says, "I have to be near the water, wherever I am. Whatever I'm doing has to be near the water. Maybe the future for me is in building these models. That would be a switch, wouldn't it? Building models instead of the real boats?" He could set up a little woodworking shop nearby at Lumpkins's Marina, where the oyster packing house used to be and where the "Connie Francis" and the "Poppa Francis" are tied up for sale at a creaky pier in a shallow cove off the St. Mary's River.

The Curtis Brothers Sail Loft, Oxford ～

Most Maryland sail lofts are not sail *lofts* in the truest sense—an attic-like space with a wide, open hardwood floor where sails are laid out, and pinned down without the aid of electronic equipment. The modern operation still requires floor space, but often it is on a ground floor and sails are designed by computers and cut from synthetic fabrics by lasers.

At Downes Curtis Sailmakers, however, the designing, cutting, assembly, and sewing are still done solely by hand, in a loft on the second floor of the old Oxford School classroom where brothers Downes, 81, and Albert, 76, sat many years ago as students. The loft has been here nearly fifty years, and the school existed many years before that.

The windows are curtainless because the brothers work mainly with natural light, with bare light bulbs hanging from the ceiling over old sewing machines and modern gooseneck lamps used to illuminate close-up work.

Strangers to this lovely old Eastern Shore yachting town on the Tred Avon River have a problem finding the old sail loft because there is no sign on this unmarked, unnumbered Tilghman Street building. Today, Oxford, founded in 1683, is a tidy village of well-off retirees, although a few active boatyards continue to do exemplary work.

"We both started cutting sails as teenagers for an old English sailmaker, David Pritchett, who died in 1936," says Downes. "We cut canvas sails for log canoes and oyster-dredging boats, you know, skipjacks and bugeyes. If they didn't get sails from us, they got them from Mr. Brown in Deal Island. Mr. Brown is gone. Only us is left who does it the old-timey way." The Oxford-born Curtis brothers also cut sails for their oyster-dredging father, Raphael.

They used to make sails of Egyptian cotton for the pleasure-seeking yachties who frequented Ralph Wiley's famous boatyard in Oxford. "We still have bolts of that cotton, should someone want sails of that material," says Albert. "But no one does anymore. We went from canvas to cotton to nylon to dacron. We still do a lot of canvas work, but only for covers, not sails."

The loft, up a creaky stairway, measures 20 by 35 feet. The hardwood floor is rough, unfinished, and punctured by a million pin holes. Peeling walls are left unpainted and are plastered with notes, pictures, and calendars. Fabric, equipment, supplies, and old sailmaking tools from the early twentieth century hang from hooks and are scattered about on tables. It is a wonderful jumble of years of accumulated things that are still in use. "We were going to put down plywood to cover this here old beat-up floor," says Downes, "but our customers said if we did they would take their business elsewhere. We listened to them, not us."

Long wooden tables lie empty, in wait for strips of canvas or dacron, where Downes or Albert will feed the material while the other sews it. There are no family members to succeed them in the business. "You can't find no one who wants to take the time anymore to learn how to do it right," says Downes. "This ain't like making a dress, you know."

The Meshach Browning Fishing Camp, Grantsville ⌣

A small sign along old Route 40 by the side of River Road, a few miles east of Grantsville in Garrett County, tells it all: "MARYLAND'S LAST BEST KEPT SECRET. MESHACH BROWNING CLUB." It was an enticing reason to hang an immediate hard right onto the little blacktop road parallel to the Casselman River—a burbling, rock-filled, mountain trout stream.

A quarter-mile into what looks like no-trespassing country, a reassuring sign bids "Public Welcome." A left turn into an old hemlock grove, heavily padded with pine needles, leads to a dirt parking lot in front of a rambling, tarpaper-roofed log cabin with a stone chimney. A Budweiser sign offers an inviting hint that perhaps this isolated cabin really is open to the public.

The Meshach Browning Fishing Camp is a throwback to a less-mobile era, when fishermen returned time and again to their favorite fishing hole. Today, many anglers have recreational vehicles and trailered bass boats that take them away from the old haunts to explore new fishing possibilities. "It's the same with the old deer hunting camps," says veteran outdoor writer Bill Burton, of Baltimore. "Fishermen don't return over and over again to the same happy fishing grounds the way they used to. They get around. They're restless and seek new challenges. The old days of renting a rowboat for a day of fishing are disappearing. They're more into bass fishing these days, and they drive all over the place to get there and get a chance at winning some big cash prizes."

Asked if he had ever fished at the old Browning camp, Burton said, "I was there years and years ago. It's not still open, is it?" Mike Sawyer, a Western Maryland outdoors writer, had never even heard of the place.

Opened in the mid-1920s, the camp attracted mostly locals and an occasional fisherman-tourist traveling the old National Pike who was lured off the beaten track by the temptress river to drop his lure for a spell. Today's tourist zooms by on a national freeway that bypasses everything.

The camp, bar, and 2½ acres of grounds are owned and operated by a friendly, laid-back native of the region who "came home" and bought the place in 1979. "I wanted to find something to do that I enjoyed," explains Rheba Cofiell, 71. "I love to fish, so I figured, why not buy the old fishing camp?"

Today she lives in a wing of the 1923-vintage log cabin, built as a hunting and fishing lodge. There is a ten-stool bar, a "NO PROFANITY" sign, a jukebox (country music only), pool table, stone fireplace and wood-burning heating stove, a mounted squirrel, and deer heads and antlers. She sells longneck Budweiser for $1.25 a bottle and occasionally serves up venison as free bar snacks, along with the occasional pizza.

The picnic grounds and adjoining stream are open to anyone, free of charge, and there is a river-front cabin that rents for $125 a month (yes, a *month*) and a trailer that goes for $75 a month. Mrs. Cofiell, a widow, is not in this for the money.

"I like the company," she says, her Scottie terrier, Killer, barking at her side. "They can camp here free in their own campers and bring their own coolers of beer, as long as they don't trash the place. I'm not going to police them. I just expect them to treat it like home. Hell, every summer I even throw a free pig roast with live country music and beer."

Fly fishermen, many of them regulars, sometimes cook their trout on a skillet set up right by the stream during the "keeper" part of the season. Some use cane rods and carry creel baskets lined with river grass.

An office worker for many years and far removed from her old River Road home, she lives (and works) in the cabin her father helped build. "I love the peace and quiet, but I love the people, too," she says. Her bar is open six days a week, from 10 a.m. to around midnight, although she has a 2 a.m. license.

Who was Meshach Browning? Ask that question in these parts and people will laugh. Almost every outdoorsman has a copy (the older the better) of his book, "Forty-Four Years in the Life of a Hunter." A Garrett County pioneer, his grave is near McHenry and is marked by a state marker that claims he "killed 2,000 deer and 500 bear." He died at the age of 78 in 1859. Too bad. Meshach Browning would have loved this fishing camp named after him.

The Original Historic Little Wedding Chapel, Elkton ⌢

Elkton has never quite been able to shake its national reputation as the place to get married in a hurry, no questions asked, even though that's not true anymore. Dating back to the 1930s, the town really was a notorious marriage mill, with dozens of greedy, marrying parsons available on twenty-four-hour call. Highway billboards blatantly hawked the quickie wedding, and shameless hustlers, commissioned by so-called justices of the peace, battled with rival marriage pimps at bus and railroad depots over each matrimonial prize. Especially during the boom years of World War II, blissful pairs, sober and drunk, were herded like cattle in and out of tacky "chapels" and then to highway "honeymoon motels." But Babe Ruth was married here, as were Bette Davis, Ethel Merman, Nixon's attorney general John Mitchell and Martha, and television evangelist Pat Robertson, to name a few.

Today, all those cutely rigged "chapels" have vanished, except for "The Original Historic Little Wedding Chapel" on Main Street, conveniently located right across the street from the Cecil County Courthouse, where marriage licenses are still issued without a blood test.

The beautiful fieldstone chapel dates from the late eighteenth century, and its square windows are "arched" on the interior by plastic cutouts, which give it a chapel-like look. A pink canopied awning hangs over the front door, and a large pale pink sign in gothic lettering fixed to the center of the building reads: "Chapel." Inside, however, the one-room chapel smells of mildew and is still a bit on the tacky side. There are two potted palms, an arched window painted to look like stained glass, and six two-person plywood "pews" done in a light mahogany stain. A floor candelabrum holds fourteen candles, and a basket of flowers sits on the boxy "altar," slightly raised on a carpeted platform.

Conducting the perfectly legal wedding ceremonies is Karin Pasqualini, 29, of Newark, Delaware, an "ordained minister" of the mail-order Universal Life Church. She holds a blank book that looks something like a Bible but contains only the words to four ceremonies. "We don't play 'Here Comes the Bride' music but rather a very tasteful organ recording of a processional march," she says. "Some ask to leave the word *God* out of it. I usually start out with something like 'We have come together to witness.' It's all over in about ten minutes."

Barbara Foster, who once operated a dance studio, bought the chapel thirteen years ago with the idea of turning it into an antiques shop. "But I came to enjoy the weddings and I'm even thinking of opening a chapel in Baltimore," she says. Mrs. Foster is a no-nonsense, fast-talking woman who has "seen it all," she says. "I had a dog for a best man once; gay weddings; biker weddings; and a Mafia wedding with bodyguards stationed outside. No, never had a nudist wedding. I wouldn't go for that." Mostly, it's just your average Joe Six-Pack out to save a few bucks.

"Maryland now has a two-day waiting period, but no blood tests are required," she says, a little bit weary of being interviewed by newspaper reporters and batting out the kind of quick answers they want to hear. "We've married a girl of 14 (with paternal consent), and a man in his late 80s to a girl in her early 20s," she says. "Tears? Sure! We get tears for the right reasons, and for the wrong reasons. Brides in an advanced state of pregnancy? That's the name of the game!"

"Many people still think they can dash over here and get married immediately at any time of the day or night. I get calls at two o'clock in the morning from couples in Atlantic City who have obviously had a little too much to drink. I tell them to think it over and call me back in the morning and we'll go over the details. They don't always call back."

While most of the marriages are ordinary affairs with well-dressed couples of all ages, there is no escaping the fact that some think getting married at Elkton's Original Historic Little Wedding Chapel is the funky thing to do.

Mrs. Foster is a little bit offended that church-going townspeople look down on her operation as a continuation of a tradition they'd rather forget. "It's not a fly-by-night operation anymore," she adds. "There are rules and regulations, and I follow 'em all to the letter. Look, we don't marry locals anyway so it's not like we take away any church business."

She says she hosts maybe nine hundred marriages a year and that her best day is (naturally) Valentine's Day, when thirty or more couples take advantage of the date. "They come here on Halloween, too," she says. "I once saw two costumed vampires get married. At least I *hope* they were wearing costumes!"

Use of the chapel is $85 on weekdays until 4:30 p.m. The rate goes up to $125 after 4:30 and on Saturdays. Sunday marriages fetch $150. Videos and still photographs can be arranged, but a chapel reception is limited to B.Y.O.B. After that—as in all weddings large and small, grand and not-so-grand—it's good luck, out the door, and you're on your own, baby.

Silenced Pipe Organ Plant, Hagerstown ⁓

A prime example of a vanishing industry in Maryland was the sad demise of the Möller pipe organ plant in Hagerstown. Built in 1895, it was clearly a survivor from another era, with its rambling, penitentiary-like plant and its exquisite, hand-crafted organs, which soared physically and spiritually within its industrial brick walls. Its neighborhood must have been great to work in, with the organ tunings booming out of the spooky old building, which stretched for two blocks and resembled a nineteenth-century mill.

The largest pipe organ plant in the world, the M. P. Möller Company built "from scratch" more pipe organs (12,000) than any other organ builder between 1877 and 1992, when production ceased, with millions of dollars of orders still on the books. The company was a victim of recessionary times, management changes, inefficiency, and labor disputes. A series of bankruptcy auctions in January 1993 laid bare the agony of this vanishing industry, trapped in the very act of vanishing, literally piece by piece. Everything went on the auction block—from pencil sharpeners and clocks to 70,000 board feet of kiln-dried lumber and a newly completed M. P. Möller chandelier pipe organ.

"It's a historic moment in the life of a historic industry that has come to an end," said Ronald Schlotterbeck, one of the first bidders, who bought a $20 box of safety goggles, hardly a piece of historic memorabilia. Of the thousands of woodworkers, machinists, sentimentalists, pipe organ experts from around the world, and just plain curious folks, the most-watched bidders were the representatives of Paul Stuck's King of Instruments chain stores of Chicago.

This firm had paid $50,000 for the Möller name, customer lists, records, blueprints, and trade secrets. "Möller shall rise like a Phoenix from the ashes," Stuck said, announcing plans to continue to build new Möller organs and repair old ones in Hagerstown, although not in the outdated old plant.

The three-story, 130,000-square-foot plant was a warren of rooms, large and small, that performed every conceivable (and some inconceivable) function of putting together some of the largest and finest pipe organs in the world. From a foundry in the basement to sheet metal storage rooms, these highly complex musi-

cal instruments, costing as much as $1 million each, emerged during a creative process requiring thousands of minute technical steps.

The organs were completely assembled and tuned to perfection in a gigantic final assembly room the size of an indoor sports arena before being disassembled for shipping. Ironically, it was in this room of final glory that the first day of the final disassembly of all that glory began—to the babbling tune of an auctioneer.

A two-hour-long tour through the plant the day before the three-day auction was a mind-boggling experience, leaving visitors stricken with astonishment and wonder over how this product was ever put together. "I still get lost in this cavernous place," said a guide from the local J. G. Cochran Auctioneering Company. "It took us eight months to sort things out," he said of the hundreds of thousands of items used in the production of these pipe organs—machinery fallen silent and covered with dust and cobwebs.

It all began in the late nineteenth century with one ambitious man from Denmark. Mathias Petter Möller was one of the country's rare organbuilders whose firm lasted more than a century in a fascinating but frustrating business. Möller, a knight of the Ancient Order of Danneborg, who died in 1937, was smitten by the art of organbuilding in 1854 as a nine-year-old apprenticed to a master in Copenhagen. In 1872 he came to America to build organs and in 1880 moved to Hagerstown, where he built his first plant, subsequently enlarged six times.

A disastrous fire in 1895 nearly wiped him out, but he built a new plant, on Prospect Street, and again had to enlarge the quarters many times. He soon began making all his own pipework and by the early 1920s had modernized his operation from tubular-pneumatic action to electro-pneumatic action.

Möller was not an organist, but he did play the violin. A man of many interests, he even began manufacturing luxury automobiles (the Dagmar) and Möller taxicabs. He was succeeded by his son, M. P. Möller, Jr., who died in 1961. A brother-in-law, W. Riley Daniels, associated with the firm for thirty years, then took over.

John J. Tyrrell, an organ architectural consultant who was once associated with Möller, wrote, "Creating an object of beauty can be tremendously satisfying, but there are many snares along the path of organbuilding: changes in musical tastes and in religious thinking and practice, national and personal economic disasters, in-house personality clashes, the risk of experimentation with new material or methods, labor disputes, and artistic caprices. . . ." By 1989 a group of specialists in industrial management, corporate engineering, and financial planning were in charge of the Möller business. In early 1990, Tyrrell observed: "Möller's future seems even brighter than it has been for many years" and there were ambitious "plans to construct a new, efficient plant."

But it was too late. One visit to the plant's lumber mill made an outsider wonder how they ever did it—all that wood and all those lengths and thicknesses: birch, walnut, poplar, maple, fir, cherry, ash, mahogany, ponderosa pine, red and white oak.

But Möller craftsmen see some hope in the fact that the Möller name at least may survive; even if the plant and all its contents have been sold and spread around the world. There is, of course, no way that a Möller pipe organ can ever be put together again in the old Möller way. Those days are gone.

In a way, though, the heart and soul of this operation will survive the recession, the mismanagement, the labor disputes, and all the inefficiencies connected with trying to make a dinosaur of a plant function at the end of the twentieth century. They survive in a glorious, timeless fashion because its organ music soars to the heavens. If you wish to witness the magic of Möller, you can hear its legacy at the U.S. military academies of the army, navy, and air force; at the Church of St. Paul the Apostle and the Lincoln Center in New York City; the National Shrine of the Immaculate Conception in Washington; the Cathedral of Mary Our Queen in Baltimore; and at many other locations around the country.

Eyler's Valley Chapel, Emmitsburg ⌣

What lures people to the little Eyler's Valley Chapel in the woods of Western Maryland is not necessarily the power of the Lord or powerful preaching. What seems to bring them to the nondenominational, early evening Sunday services is candlepower; the flickering of dozens of candles inside glass chimney lamps creates a glow in the night.

There are, of course, many churches in Maryland that partially depend upon candlelight to cast a hushed spell of solemnity over religious services. But few churches rely solely on candlepower for light as well as for spiritual enhancement as does this little stone chapel nestled in a dark and peaceful valley a few miles west of Emmitsburg.

Built in 1857, this one-room country chapel by the side of the road has never been invaded by the shock of electricity or the rumblings of indoor plumbing and central heating. And, because of the chapel's updated by-laws, this serene way of life will never experience the harshness of artificial lighting or the indoor comforts of flush toilets, hot air heat, and air conditioning.

Perhaps the best time of year to experience this disappearing wonder is during the Christmas season. The drive to the isolated chapel along Eyler's Valley Flint Road is over a mountainous dirt road through a dark and sometimes menacing woods. Only auto headlights guide the way until the friendly patch of flickering light is spotted.

The chapel in the dell, with a stream meandering through its backyard and an old cemetery waiting patiently on a nearby hillside, is a beacon of welcome as well as a spiritual ray of hope.

The chapel can cast a spell over the most determinedly fallen-away worshiper, and combining that sight with the sounds of a tolling church bell and voices singing "Oh, Come All Ye Faithful" is enough to put a lump in anyone's throat.

The leader of this informal flock is Kenneth Hamrick, 54, a minister with the nearby Thurmont Methodist Church. "I had heard about this then-abandoned church in Eyler's Valley in the summer of 1969 and thought I'd drive over and take a look at it," he says. "I expected to find a building in shambles, but it wasn't in bad shape. It seemed that it was closed in the 1920s, again in the 1940s, and then

sort of abandoned. Since it was once affiliated with the Methodist church in Thurmont, I volunteered to hold a trial daytime service there. We had 19 people show up at that first service in September of 1969, and that went on until we switched to Sunday evening services in March of 1971."

The candlelight service triggered an immediate response, and soon 85 people were arriving. During December, a series of twelve night services began drawing as many as 188, packing the little church to such a human capacity that the two portable gas heaters were hardly needed.

"We now have a total of 80 candles," says Hamrick, who also looked after the installation of little wooden footbridges over the brook, an outdoor privy, and an open-sided pavilion in the backyard where picnics and receptions are held. The church has also become a highly popular setting for romantic, candlelit weddings.

"Everything defies reason here," observes Hamrick. "Reopening an abandoned church on a lonely dirt road in the middle of the mountains? And packing them in every Sunday evening, even drawing people from out-of-state? Somehow, I like to think that there is a higher power at work here than candlepower."

Reliable Weavers, Baltimore ⌣

When a garment finally shows signs of wearing out, most people will simply toss it, give it away, or take it to a consignment shop. But some, when confronted with fashionable shabbiness overtaking a favorite item of apparel, will seek the professional services of a weaver—a reliable weaver.

Such a reliable weaver was "Bud" Weiner, of Reliable Weavers, at 212 West Saratoga Street, who continued the tradition of weaving that had survived in this Baltimore block for more than seventy years. Here they mended garments that people simply could not bear to part with. One of the shop's customers was President Herbert Hoover, who was attached to a particular suit with a hole in it.

"This is not patchwork stitching, such as what you might get at a tailor's or a dry cleaning shop. It is French weaving," he said when interviewed, before he retired and closed his little shop in 1992. "It is meticulous, tedious work, usually done through a large magnifying glass, thread by thread, exacting and precise," he added, demonstrating his craft in a dimly lit back room. "We match the thread with the weave and we don't stop until we get it exact. It's not cheap. You have to really love a garment to go through this, especially if it's a $1,500 Italian suit that would be folly to throw away."

Weiner prefers not revealing his age and prefers being called Bud, the name by which he was listed in the Yellow Pages under "Weaving and Mending Service." His shop was the last in the city devoted solely to weaving, with no side lines of tailoring or dry cleaning. The narrow little shop, with the weaving workroom in back, had two chairs nestled in a sunny front window alcove overlooking the busy sidewalk, where Weiner took the time to chat with customers over coffee. Hurrying was not part of his Old World ways.

"If the work is perfect, as our work was, even the owner, who knew where the hole had been, could not find it after we finished with it," he said proudly. The hole simply vanished when these vanishing weavers performed their specialized magic.

Framed letters from delighted customers decorated the walls and filled a scrapbook that Weiner enjoyed showing off. The unsolicited letters of thanks were often effusive testimonials from hard-nosed business executives who had actually taken the time to show their genuine, heart-felt appreciation.

"Sometimes we received a garment accompanied by a blank, signed check with a plea to do whatever was required to save it," he said. "They believed in our service and in our slogan," he said, pointing to a sign near his front counter that stated: "What is Impossible to Others is Possible to Us."

Before polyester and double knits came on the scene in the early 1970s, Weiner employed as many as fourteen highly skilled weavers, many of whom worked at home. "One of my weavers, Edna Finnegan, who has passed away, did weaving work for more than sixty-five years," said Weiner. "She was always sewing and knitting, even on the way home. Weavers and knitters have to keep their hands moving. Good weavers are hard to find these days," he added, "so I prefer not to give out their names because, to me, that is like revealing a professional secret even if I'm not using them anymore. They are getting old, like me, and young people are not interested in taking it up. I can tell you about Edna because she's dead."

The business was founded in 1919 as Reliable Weavers by Anne Barry, who was in her seventies when she retired to Florida and sold the operation in 1946 to the Weiner brothers, Bud and Paul. They bought the shop after they left the army, on the advice of their father, a maker of fur coats who preferred working with individual customers rather than manufacturers. Anne Barry taught the young Weiner boys the fine art of weaving, although Paul later turned to the practice of law.

"She had her own secret list of homebound weavers and their names went with the business," said Weiner, who sold his business and the building at 212 and retired the name Reliable Weavers. He gave his old neon sign and some store items to the Baltimore Museum of Industry where he may, or may not, make himself available from time to time to demonstrate what it was that a weaver did—"if anyone is interested," he said.

Oak Splint Basket Makers since 1876, North East ⌒

At the Day Basket Company, in North East, little has changed in the method of making tough, durable, beautiful, and utilitarian baskets of raw white oak that has been steamed, sawn and stripped. The craftspeople are not old-timers bent over in their work, but they've been trained in the old ways to produce a functional basket that lasts, rather than a cheap, dyed, throwaway reed basket designed to hold nothing heavier than chocolate cream Easter eggs.

Basketmaking brothers Edward and Samuel Day, of Massachusetts, set up operations in 1876, near a Susquehanna River landing. They shipped their baskets from here to the southern market for use by cotton pickers. The company is now owned by Robert F. McKnight, a former North East powerboat dealer who bought the business in 1989 shortly before the boating industry went into a decline. He feels more secure with baskets than with boats, because baskets, after all, have a longer history of survival—going back to antiquity.

The Day Company has been operating in its present location, near the railroad tracks just off Route 40, since the early 1900s, surviving two major fires in the 1940s. But where there once were thirty-five people turning out 2,000 baskets a week during World War I, the plant now employs five craftspeople who produce some 7,000 a year.

The native white oak arrives in "flitch-cut" slices from logs, and is sawn and softened by steaming in a wood-fired steam box. From there, it is clamped to a workbench where the strips are cut off and split into long strips with a draw knife, producing "stanups" and "fillers."

The stanups are used for the bottom and framework of the basket. The hoops strengthening the mouth of the basket are sawn, rather than split. An inside hoop is made around a form and then steamed and nailed into shape before the weaving process begins.

After the sides are woven, in and out in a basket pattern, the weaver wraps an outside hoop around the inside hoop and fastens both hoops with copper nails. After handles are installed, yokes are laced under the filler for reinforcement. Some baskets are further strengthened with iron strapping.

The baskets made by Day Company have changed little in design since the firm's beginning. They now range in price from $18 to $80 and are sold throughout the country. "We've had people come in here who tell us they've been using their Day baskets for 30 and 40 years," says McKnight, who is manager, administrator, chief executive officer, and president—but not a basketmaker. "We make lunch, picnic, market, berry, fruit, bread, pie, picking, waste, laundry, mail, firewood, and baby baskets," he says. "But people find all sorts of uses for our baskets."

Visitors may tour the basket factory six days a week. The production time from board to basket is forty minutes, and an experienced weaver can produce about twenty-five baskets a day. If you have forty minutes to kill, you can actually track your own basket from log to finished basket.

The Martin Wagner Blacksmith Shop, Rock Hall ⁓

When an official road marker honors a commercial establishment as a historical site, the only thing remaining of the honoree is often a collapsing chimney overgrown with weeds. The business is usually history. But in Rock Hall, across the street from an iron, black-lettered marker pointing out "The Old Martin Wagner Blacksmith Shop (1899-1980) on Route 20, the old blacksmith shanty is not only still there, it's still in business and being run by a member of the Wagner family.

During the winter, it may not look as if it's actually open, because the shed doors may be closed. But if wood smoke is curling out of the stovepipe, the hospitable Alfred Jacquette, 64, is sure to be working somewhere in the dimly lit interior. This is a blacksmith and welding shop in the purest sense, unlike the more tidy shops of the newcomer smithies specializing in knives, iron scrollwork, and fancy fences. The Martin Wagner Blacksmith Shop does anything and everything when it comes to ironwork. It is one hell of a mess; an accumulation of decades of indifferent storage solutions. There is no kinder way to say it.

"We don't have no display counter or no over-the-counter stock items on hand, unless you're looking for an oyster culling hammer, because we do keep those in stock," says Jacquette, whose large stomach is usually drooping over a thigh-high anvil as he pounds away on some piece of iron.

"People come in here dragging broken things, or with a sketch of something, to tell me what they want made or fixed, and that's what I give them," he adds. "Oh yeah, I still fire up the forge like Mr. Martin and Mr. Harry used to do."

"Mr. Martin" was the Martin Wagner (1899-1980) mentioned on the historical marker. He learned the trade from his father, "Mr. Harry" (Harrison E. Wagner), who died in 1955 at the age 83. Mr. Harry worked under *his* father, William Wagner, who took over what was an existing blacksmith shop in the early 1860s. "Mr. William" died in 1922 at the age of 81. Martin taught the trade to son-in-law Jacquette, who began working at the shop full-time thirty-six years ago.

Jacquette may be the last family member to carry on the blacksmithing tradition, because his son is only interested in auto mechanics, not welding. "I'll keep doing it as long as I can, just like my wife's people did," he says. "She says I had better, because she don't want me hanging around the house. I agree. I don't want too, neither. Besides, I like the shop. I get to see all my friends here when they stop by on their rounds to nowhere and back again."

Two-thirds of his work is still done for watermen, who find it more economical to have something repaired rather than to replace it. They especially like his five-pronged grappling hooks and old-fashioned, two-fluke anchors, used for holding workboats over hard bottoms.

"The way it looks for the future, with the seafood harvest declining, I might have to get into the iron trinket business, like making supports for mail boxes or turning my grappling hooks into flower pot holders," he says, laughing.

During World War II, when parts and supplies were hard to get, Mr. Martin and Mr. Harry kept the farmers and watermen in business by making whatever was needed, Jacquette explained. "They'd even make 'house calls' to the farms, if they had to. I'm a jack-of-all-trades farmboy and mechanically inclined, too."

The shed-like, Kent County shop at the corner of Route 20 and Martin Wagner Road has a leaning, rusted tin roof and is covered with tarpaper in a red brick design. In the summer, weeds and vines try to take over the building, which has an abandoned look to it. Whatever it may lack, it does not lack personality.

The character of this Upper Eastern Shore shop has been developed and refined over a 140-year period. There is not a square foot of floor that is not covered by tools and raw material, in some cases piled so high that cautious visitors prefer to remain outside, where the light and smells are better. "If anyone started moving things around here other than me, I couldn't find it again, which of course happens all the time anyway," says Jacquette.

The girlie posters hanging on the walls are vintage auto parts calendar art, and some of them date to the 1960s and earlier. The "boys" who hang around here don't consult the calendars for the days and dates of years past, but they do gaze at the portraits.

The portly blacksmith stands 5 feet 7 inches, weighs 265 pounds, and insists on driving the quarter-mile home for lunch rather than walking. "I gave up chewing tobacco and smoking cigars, but ain't no way I'm gonna give up food for exercise," he says. His hair is often unkempt and tousled, especially in the summer, when a few fans blow the hot air around, although there is a cross breeze from a nearby field when the shed doors are open. "It gets hot in here sometimes," he says —especially when sparks from his welding torch burn holes through his shirts and trousers and singe his skin.

Tourists generally believe the shed is a vanished part of local history, says Jacquette. They may glance over and, if the door is open for the cross breeze, might even peek inside to see what's going on in the darkness. "One time I overheard a guy talking about 'the old blacksmith shop' and wondering about when they was going to tear this place down because nothing was going on inside there no more," says Jacquette. "I laughed and told him *I* was going on inside there and not to start tearing it down while I'm still inside."

Jacquette's wife, Anna Ruth, says she's going to get "my Alfred" to hang some of his old-fashioned, handmade anchors outside the shed door facing Route 20 and "put up an 'Anchors for Sale' sign, even if they'd use 'em for nothing but hanging flower pots. And after I got him to do that," she continues, "I'm gonna get him to start walking home for lunch and back for the exercise."

Alfred Jacquette walking home to lunch? Alfred Jacquette making anchors for flower pot hangers? That'll be the day.

Last of the Cooperages, Cambridge ⌒

One may still find a wooden Brooks barrel used to ship a product into Maryland, but there aren't many new Brooks barrels used to ship much of anything out of Maryland except for some coffee beans and crab claws. Brooks Barrel Company, the last cooperage in Maryland, still makes barrels from yellow pine trees cut on the Eastern Shore and trucked to its Cambridge plant, where they are sawn, cut, beveled into staves, and cured in storage. But these barrels, still made by hand with the aid of antique machinery, are now used mostly as decorative flower pots and display containers.

At one time, almost everything was shipped and stored in barrels: vegetables, seafood, meat, flour, sugar, powdered milk, molasses, spices, alcohol, hardware. Most of these items are now shipped in rugged, waxed, water-resistant cardboard boxes. The barrels became too expensive, and were too heavy and clumsy to store and handle. Barrels now serve as planters, chairs, fancy trash receptacles, decorative kegs and buckets of varying sizes, and to display and stow hard rock candy, apples, potatoes, seed, magazines, laundry, firewood, umbrellas, coals.

"Our barrels provide that old-timey flavor," says Ken Knox, 39, of Cambridge, who bought the 43-year-old Brooks Barrel Company in 1990 from founder Paul Brooks, also of Cambridge. "They look good, smell good, and they can take a lot of abuse," adds partner Mike Knopp, 39. "They are sturdier than the shipping barrels, which are built lighter and usually discarded soon after use."

When Brooks, 71, got into the cooperage business in 1950 about a half-dozen other cooperages were building "slack" (not water-tight) barrels in Maryland. Today, this is one of the few slack cooperages left in the entire country. James T. Warring and Sons, a Washington cooperage begun in 1918 and now located in Prince George's County, no longer makes barrels but still deals in used, reconditioned whiskey barrels.

"When I went into this business more than forty years ago, I was warned the slack cooperage trade was dying," says Brooks. "But it's still going strong, if you go in the right direction with it. The thing with doing business is that times change and you must change with them and adapt to survive. We survived." About 75 percent of Brooks barrels are used for planters and sold in lawn and garden shops in fourteen states.

Inside the plant, across from the Cambridge Airport, the racket that goes into the making of a barrel is deafening. Fewer than a dozen men assemble the barrels, and most of them are under 50 years of age. But the way of making these barrels has remained unchanged for decades.

The staves (barrel side slats) are machine-cut to exacting measurements and set into a forming ring. Deft handling, like fitting the pieces of a puzzle, brings them together tightly to form a full circle with flared-out staves. The cooper then drops a cable around the staves, which pop together, making a neatly symmetrical shape.

Next, a strange machine called "the five-in-one" slips the metal hoops in place. A crozier whizzes around the inside of the rigid, open-ended barrel, cutting grooves for the heads and bottoms, which are then secured in place.

The plant annually turns out tens of thousands of barrel products of all sizes. Crabbers, for example, continue to drop their catches from pots (traps) and trot lines into bushel baskets, which are trucked away at boat landings. Some Baltimore crab houses still use the large Brooks barrels to transport steamed crabs locally. Knox and Knopp also make washtubs with cut-out handholds, buckets with iron hoop handles, and barrels with holes in the sides used as strawberry planters. "The future of slack barrels is in planters," says Knox.

It's an odd fate when you think about it: barrels once used to transport things grown in fields are now being filled with field dirt and used to grow things.

Dee Herget, Screen Painter, Essex ⌒

Window and door screens hand-painted with bucolic, Disney-like cartoon land-scapes are as traditional to East Baltimore's brick row houses as white marble steps. But as the practitioners of this folk art retired from screenpainting or died—and a booming aluminum storm window and screen industry replaced the old painted window screens—the quaint, folksy practice slipped into decline.

The masters are dead: William and Richard Oktavec, Ben and Ted Richardson, Frank Abremski, Charles Bowman, and others. According to Baltimore folklorist and painted screen scholar Elaine Eff, "only Dee Herget can be counted on to fill a screen order on demand."

Herget, 59, of Essex, in eastern Baltimore County, proudly acknowledges that she is the only "accomplished window screen folk artist left who still advertises commercially." A blunt woman who speaks in a high, squeaky voice, she is terribly authoritarian when it comes to discussing "her" art. "There are some screen painters out there whose work is truly dreadful," she says. "But there may be some real talents working in the privacy of their homes and painting screens only for their family and friends. I do it commercially, although there doesn't seem to be as great a demand for painted window screens as there used to be. My work goes mostly to people in Essex, Dundalk, and Rosedale."

A student of Ben Richardson, Herget took up the art as a hobby in the late 1970s after being forced to retire because of a hearing problem. "I dusted. I sewed. I mended. I cleaned. I was bored to tears," she says. "I had to do something, so I enrolled in an art course, because I always liked to draw."

Since she lived in Highlandtown, a hotbed of painted screens, she had an artistic as well as a practical appreciation of them. "They not only add some trees and grass to brick walls and cement sidewalks," she explains, "but they also protect your privacy and allow you to snoop on sidewalk activity from that privacy of your own living room. You can see out, but no one can see in because of the paint."

Herget, who signs her work in the lower left hand corner, paints in a 12-by-12-foot pantry under a fluorescent lamp. "It's just my washer, dryer, me, and my screens," she says.

"Preparing the screen is important," she explains. "I use a secret paint mix that

will last. No, I ain't gonna tell you what it is! You got to use the paint sparingly, or else you'll clog the damn screen holes. I can do a couple a day, if I have the orders."

According to Eff, the neighborhood-based art was invented by William Oktavec in 1913. A Czech grocer, he painted fruits and vegetables on the screen door of his store in Baltimore's Little Bohemia. This progressed to his painting "an idyllic landscape featuring a red-roofed bungalow dwarfed by a forest of towering greenery and fluffy white clouds," she says. "The little house was perched above a winding path, leading to a pond inhabited by a family of swans."

Soon, it was all the rage and everyone within a ten-block radius had to have their own rural vision of domestic tranquility, usually improvised from greeting cards and calendar art.

Herget carries on that tradition today. "I have my own version of the RB [red-roofed bungalow]," she says, also referring to her generic version as "my fairytale cottage in the country." She charges from $15 to $20 to paint a screen. "That's if you bring your own mounted screen, you understand."

She uses a thatched red roof, white birch trees, a stone-lined pond with flower beds and a pair of resident white swans. It has a soothing, innocent look to it, as in Snow White and the Seven Dwarves. "The only difference is, most of those who have these painted screens still live in the city in brick row houses with cement lawns and barely a tree in sight," Herget explains.

"Not me!" she adds. "I got away from all that and found real bucolic escape beyond the painted screen. I live in a little bungalow in Rockaway Beach with white aluminum siding and black shutters. I have trees, flowers, and ducks and I can see Sue Creek across the road. That's pretty close to my dream RB, I'd say."

But even though she has achieved the painted window screen fantasy and is now living in the tranquil setting of her own art, she still resides behind her own painted window screens—just in case something goes wrong with the dream.

Cropper's Small Mall, Shelltown ⌒

The fabled country stores of Norman Rockwell's calendar art are fast disappearing from Maryland's rural landscape, victims of the convenience stores, supermarkets, shopping centers, and automobiles that take shoppers away from the neighborhood. In recent years, many of these crossroads landmarks have been put up for sale, shut down, or abandoned to weeds. But Billy Cropper's tiny one-room wood-frame store in Shelltown (pop. 35)—its rusted and sagging tin roof shading a creaky little front porch—is a one-of-a-kind classic. Not really a store, it survives solely through Billy's indomitable will to preserve his haunting memories of growing up and working in this store and in his father's large general store.

This white-washed shack, on the Lower Eastern Shore in Somerset County, still has horse collars and harnesses hanging in a back room. It sits on Shelltown Road near where it dead-ends at a Pocomoke River landing. There are fewer than a dozen houses in downtown Shelltown.

The store has a closed look to it, except for a waggish modern sign ("Cropper's Small Mall") that a city admirer on a lark gave Cropper to hang next to his battered screened door. An occasional tourist will peek inside, and some are brave enough to actually enter and face down the stares of the Cropper regulars who will, at first, immediately clam up.

"Rightly speaking, this ain't hardly no store at all," explains Cropper, 65, a bachelor and the last member of his family to work and live in Shelltown. "This is a meeting place for hanging out; not a place to make money." He keeps it open purely for sentimental reasons, and "to fight loneliness and keep from going crazy with nothing to do since I gave up feeesh-ing."

A dour, sullen-looking man with a close crew cut and a pot belly, he does not appear over-friendly, but he is actually a warm and welcoming fellow with a delightfully pure Shore twang. He has an impish sense of humor about the place and appreciates the fact that it is a totally obsolete anachronism. On sale are cigarettes, chewing tobacco (he is a regular user), soda pop, Lance crackers, and frozen Reese's peanut butter cups and Milky Ways. There are some dust-covered goods and merchandise stored on the cluttered shelves, but mostly the place is filled with items placed there randomly years ago and forgotten.

Cropper even keeps a traditional country store "day book," in which he records charges to the few accounts still maintained, more out of tradition than anything else. But this is one service being phased out, as indicated by a hand-lettered sign: "Starting Wed Nov 11 there will be no charging of anything over two weeks at a time." Another sign goes into more complicated detail over store charge policies.

On the front door is another crude sign: "If store is closed and you want to get in blow horn or come to back steps and call." He lives next door in the home the Croppers built in the late 1920s when Billy was a toddler. He continues to keep his home phone listed in the name of his father, T. F. Cropper, who died 41 years ago.

Billy retired in 1989 after thirty years with a local feed and chicken company. For a long while he "looked after" his unmarried sister, Leanna, who worked in the store for years before she died in 1992 at the age of 76. His fondest memories are of growing up and working at the big Cropper General Store in Shelltown before "a twister" tore it down fifty-two years ago. "It was then that my father bought this here store, in 1941," he says. "It used to be on the river, for a hundred years or more, until they moved it here, and here it's been ever since and here it will stay as long as *I'm* here."

Cropper sits in a folding metal chair near the back of the store, facing the front door. To his right is a propane gas stove that replaced a potbellied stove, and a tin can for spitting tobacco juice. Several upturned wooden crates serve as places to sit, and against the wall is a long, battered seatbench containing bins once filled with large house nails.

On the counter is a "Dewald" radio and record player his father gave Billy as a little boy. "The radio still works, but not the record player," he says. "I took the record player apart many, many years ago and could never get the thing back together again. That's the way it's been ever since—broke." On a back counter sits an old porcelain Toldeo scale. It hasn't been used in a long, long time because there's nothing to weigh anymore.

Farmers stop by throughout the day, to talk of crops, politics, crops, weather, crops, politics, crops, local gossip, crops, sports, and crops. Cropper exchanges views, reads local newspapers, and watches sporting events on television (a rather formidable TV aerial wavers on the roof). He also has an interest in harness racing and even owns a race horse, which is not exactly a champion.

Along the waterfront, where a public boat-launching ramp attracts fishermen, a haul-out marine railway ("No Cash No Splash") is handy but can accommodate only one workboat at a time. Nothing else much goes on in Shelltown, and shells no longer pile up because all the old oyster-shucking houses are gone.

"We've restored the old one-room post office building over across the road," Cropper points out. "I guess you can say that's something that's going on here, but I don't know when they'll get around to finishing the inside. They got the flagpole up, though, I can tell you that—although I ain't seen the flag flying yet. About the rest of it, I can't hardly tell you much."

Harry Shaw's Gas Station, Moscow ⌒

Service stations in Maryland are not what they used to be in this impersonal, homogeneous age of pump your own gas, wipe your own windshield, and check your own oil and water or pay extra. Gone is the "friendly uniformed attendant" with the officer's cap and leather bow tie who once performed all those services automatically. Now it's hand over your payment to a gum-chewing youth behind a bulletproof-glass wall who speaks through a microphone and slides your change to you in a steel drawer.

This is decidedly not the case at Harry Shaw's Exxon Station in Moscow, the only full-service gas station between Westernport to the south and Lonaconing to the north.

Built around 1920 along Route 936 and the railroad tracks (and since bypassed by Route 36), the gas station's office has not changed much since Shaw, 83, began pumping gas here some sixty-five years ago as a teenager. Then it was an Esso station and Coolidge was President. Of course, there is a new plastic Exxon sign and three new Exxon pumps, but so far the Shaws have not been inspired by modernization overtures from Exxon, which is inclined to favor the uniform sheltered service island devoid of any personal charm.

But Shaw's pumps were sheltered by an overhanging roof long before service islands came into fashion, and he has never quite gone along with the self-service routine. He still pumps the gas himself, and will check the oil and wipe the windshield, if asked. He also has regular customers who can say: "Put it on the bill, Harry," and not have to sign anything. How long this independent operation will continue as a slow-paced antique is anyone's guess.

Shaw wears a navy blue, hooded parka in winter. He is a man of very few words, so don't look for many direct quotes here. He does enjoy talking about the great snowstorms that have hit George's Creek Valley in Western Maryland, but you have to be there. During a snowstorm the regulars show up at the station to hang out, drink coffee, and watch for the snowplow ("Here comes the snowplow," they will say).

One of the last gas stations with a stone fireplace, it incorporates a little waiting room and the "office." Coal fires have blackened the stone chimney, which now houses a stovepipe from a coal- and wood-burning stove standing in front of the old hearth. It's a good place to warm one's hands and backside.

A wooden bench is against one wall, next to a stack of tires, and an inner office is scattered with chairs, including a rocker. An old-fashioned glass and wood candy counter is sparsely stocked. Since Mrs. Jones's country store and Jenkins Saloon closed, this is the only place left in the tiny village of Moscow (about sixty homes) where you can buy anything.

Among the few attractions to outsiders are the old Laurel Run and Morrison cemeteries, although one could count Shaw's landmark Exxon station as a potential draw as a commercial artifact. Also, the 1870 Shaw Mansion, a historic house on a hill just behind the station, is being restored by Craig and Ruth Marsh, of Lonaconing, as a seven-bedroom bed and breakfast. That restoration was about the only local subject people were talking about in Moscow during the winter of 1993. True, the coal train still drives through town ("Here comes the coal train," they'll say), but it doesn't stop anymore, because the deep mining era is long over.

The history of the Moscow Exxon Station is a bit uncertain, although people recall a filling station's being there since shortly after World War I. The taciturn Shaw says he bought the station "about fifty years ago. We added the auto mechanic's bay in the mid-1950s after we stopped using the old outside grease rack."

Today, Harry's son, Ronnie, 56, is the town's only resident mechanic. He works at the station with his father and son, Craig, 26. The Shaws like it the way it is. The townspeople like it the way it is, and tourists would also like it the way it is—if they only knew where it is.

Leave it alone, Exxon.

Old Town's Old Stove Shop, Baltimore ⌐

The George J. Thaler Tinsmith and Stove Parts Shop is an island outpost at a now-lonely but once-bustling corner of commerce at Madison Street and Central Avenue in Baltimore's Old Town. All the upstairs windows of the rambling brick building are boarded shut. The business, which has been there since 1870 and is the last of its kind, is a barely surviving victim of changing times and neighborhoods. It has a forlorn, abandoned look to it; but, between 10 a.m and 2 p.m. on weekdays during the winter of 1993, a dim light glowed through the unwashed, empty store windows, from behind an ancient, high wooden counter.

Inside, a Warm Morning coal stove toasts the chilly, dusty silence. Occasionally the phone rings. "Thaler's," says Joseph Thaler, 67, the last of the Thaler stove men. Ruggedly handsome, with a square jaw and wavy white hair, he is the great-grandson of Lorenz Thaler, a German tinsmith who came to Baltimore from the Old Country in 1830 and set up his first shop nearby on Gay Street in 1860.

Although no longer listed in the Yellow Pages, Thaler's still gets calls every now and then from people looking for a stove part, usually for an antique stove. The postman also arrives daily with mostly junk mail, which Thaler piles up unopened in a corner of his battered, cluttered desk.

"Now we're an antique in the antique business," Thaler notes after explaining to a potential customer that, sorry, Thaler's isn't exactly in the business full-time any more. Most people believe the shop has been closed for years anyway—and in a way it has been, since it was isolated in a kind of redevelopment limbo in the early 1980's.

"I can hardly begin to tell you how busy this place and this neighborhood was," Thaler says. "It's a commercial ghost town now, but it was so full of life and commerce. The sidewalks were so crowded with pedestrian traffic you had to walk in the street. Look at it now," he says, staring out through an unwashed window. "We still have tons and tons of parts all over the place, from the basement to the top floor, but because of a stroke I can't even climb upstairs anymore to get to anything, even if someone wanted something, although I could still find the right bin. I just show up here hoping to keep the place from being vandalized or burned to the ground."

The Thaler firm installed many of the city's tin roofs, stove pipes, and much of its rain spouting and plumbing. They equipped kitchens and converted boilers and heating furnaces from wood and coal to kerosene, oil, natural gas, and electricity. They also sold cast iron pots and pans, lanterns, pipe fittings, hot water radiators, and all the countless thousands of spare parts and hardware needed to keep a business or home functioning.

"In this business, the customer was never right," Thaler explains, laughing about his dealings with uninformed people. "The number of parts catalogues we had here, dating back to the 1860s, was absolutely shocking, even to those of us who worked here. Our stock was overwhelming. We never threw out anything, and we knew where everything was. It was totally incomprehensible to an outsider. We had thirty people working here! Now there's only me, if you can call this working."

They communicated with one another in the building through speaking tubes and pipes, which snake all through the place. Even the gas light fixtures are still in place. A sheet metal shop was on the second floor, along with a blacksmith's forge where parts were made if they couldn't be found or ordered.

The building is a true time capsule, an industrial treasure, because it has stayed put in this one location since 1870. Relocation forces a firm to get rid of old, unwanted shop machinery, parts, office records, and out-of-date catalogues (now valued by collectors). But Thaler's not only has the antiques catalogues, it has many of the parts listed in them.

Much of this historical material, office records, and equipment has been donated to the Baltimore Museum of Industry. Even the office, where Thaler is spending his last days at the firm, will be preserved at the museum. Thaler hopes he will be able to spend some time in his reconstructed office with tour groups and museum curators, explaining what went on in the family firm where he worked for fifty years.

The history of the firm is a long and involved one, colored by personality conflicts and clashes, impossible store searches, and stories of customers and clients and their impossible demands. When Lorenz Thaler had a disabling fall from a tin roof he was installing, he turned the business over to his wife, Margareta, who ran it for years before eventually surrendering it to her son, George. George's children, Thomas and Margaret (Joseph Thaler's father and aunt) were the next Thalers to operate the business. Margaret never married; she spent her life working there, becoming president in 1948 when her brother died. She retired in the early 1970s, turning over operations to Joseph, and died in 1980. For a while in the 1970s, Joseph Thaler's son, Joseph Jr., worked at the firm.

A series of mild winters caused the business to fall behind, and in the industry profound changes were occurring in the way everything was done. The business was never able to catch up or adapt to the changing ways. For a time, a renewed interest in coal and wood stoves kept things going, but that didn't last either. "Maybe we should have gone into air conditioning," Thaler muses.

Now, its all over. The tin letters fastened to the green walls above the second floor windows and spelling out "GEORGE J. THALER" are rusting away and falling off. Weeds are climbing over the security grates covering the glass show windows that once displayed hundreds of pots, pans, kettles, chamber pots, spittoons, coal shuttles, stove pipes, and anything else that could hang from a hook or rest on a dusty shelf.

Asked how he might feel when he walks for the last time out of the family shop—a circa 1850 building housing so many memories and ghosts from the past —Thaler shrugs and does not have an immediate answer. He has an ironic sense of humor about what went on and what went wrong at this place, and is not over-whelmed by a feeling of sadness.

"I'm a Dutchman and not given to displaying sentimental feelings, so I honestly cannot answer that question until that day comes," he says. "I just don't know. Maybe I'll look back for a last time and shed a tear, but then maybe again I won't."

The Last Tack Factory, Baltimore ⌒

On the fringes of Baltimore's Little Italy, at the corner of Central Avenue and Bank Street in a once-mighty industrial part of town, one may still hear the great clanging chorus of heavy manufacturing, a sound out of the past. It is the raucous sound of row upon row of hefty, belt-driven, precision machinery chewing up raw steel and spitting out tacks and nails in a plant known locally as the tack factory.

Situated on a street still partly paved with Belgian stone blocks and criss-crossed by unused railroad tracks, the family-owned Holland Manufacturing Company has coughed up billions of the familiar bluish tacks that have landed in millions of workshops and kitchen drawers.

This last major manufacturer of tacks in the country functions in a partly modern setting, but the tack-production end of the business still operates in a bygone machine age. Some thirty brutish Mackes machines on the ground floor threaten to shake apart the sound nineteenth-century brick building, which served as a hospital for Confederate prisoners during the Civil War.

These efficient tack-making machines, most of them more than seventy-five years old, are practically irreplaceable, because no one makes them like this any-more. Members of the Holland family manage to keep them banging away by keeping a large warehouse room filled with dust-covered spares, lined up like can-nons waiting for battle. Some spare parts, however, still have to be tooled by hand in the company's blacksmith shop, at a forge equipped with antique blacksmithing tools. It is a veritable working museum of industry.

Since the factory opened, around 1890, it has employed many Italian-American residents of nearby Little Italy, some of whom have worked here for more than a half-century. The company was founded by Franklin Holland, a German-born manufacturer of nails and tacks who came to Baltimore from New England. He was succeeded by his son, Howard E. Holland, father of Richard S., 60, the cur-rent president.

Other Hollands working at the tack factory include brother Robert, his sons Stephen and Randy, and son-in-law Jim Flynn. More Hollands are waiting in the wings, although the use of tacks has diminished because of the advent of power-driven staplers.

At one time, the Holland firm had six subsidiary companies and accounted for almost 20 percent of the nation's entire output of tacks, nails, and brads. Today the firm is down to this one plant.

Most of the shipping end of the operation has been modernized, with custom packaging. One would expect that the packaging line had long been automated, but that is decidedly not the case. In a corner of the warehouse—in a new adjoining section of the building that houses the cinder block–walled offices—a dozen women in an assembly line labor methodically at wooden stalls. These women (some ear-plugged into rock and roll music) continue to weigh by hand billions of tacks, nails, and brads. In some cases, they use the same grocer's scales used by their mothers and grandmothers. "It may seem antiquated, and perhaps it is," says the president, "but we have found it to be an efficient, time-tested method of operation."

One of the packers, Dolores Jachim, 61, has been working here since she was 16. She has joined a long line of members of the Jachim, Votta, Biscotti, Russo, Gerlach, Curry, Pasqualone, Pleines, Granese, Boeri, Mezzanotte, Fica, and Romaniello clans who have worked here.

Before the tacks reach the packers, they go into a tumbler to knock off the rough edges. Wet sawdust is tossed in to burnish them before they are washed and heated, turning them the familiar gun-metal blue color. This process does not, as some people believe, sterilize the tacks. One of the reasons for this seemingly elaborate finishing of a common tack is that upholsterers traditionally place a handful of tacks in their mouths and pull them off their tongues with the magnetic end of their hammers, speeding up the tacking process.

Holland has a sense of history and tradition, which is almost unavoidable, considering his family's contribution to the tack and nail industry and the tool and hardware business, which dates to the eighteenth century in America. His grandfather, in fact, designed some of the machines that still turn out the family products.

The customer who keeps the tack factory running is you and me, casual shoppers who pick up a small pack of Holland tacks at a neighborhood hardware store, forgetting that we already have them at home. The crux of the unending demand for household tacks is that we are always buying another pack to add to our hidden collection.

That's always been the explanation for why the tack machines keep clanging away at the tack factory in Baltimore's Little Italy. If we ever start remembering where our tacks are and actually start using them, the tack factory will be doomed.

Tom Courtney, Pound-Net Fisherman, Point Lookout ⌒

Pound netting, one of the most expensive and labor-intensive industries on the Bay, has been in decline in Maryland waters, primarily for these reasons: it costs about $10,000 to rig just one of the long, elaborate fish traps; it usually requires a crew of two or three paid hands doing backbreaking work; and rockfish are crowding out the nets in a mad rush to eat bait fish, flounder, and anything else that's trapped.

The last sizeable concentration of pound netters on the Bay is in the lower Potomac River, where thirty-eight set up operations in 1992. Of the eleven Maryland netters, seven were from St. Mary's County, a decrease of three from 1991. Those who give it up go on to activities such as "party boating," carrying recreational fishermen who guarantee an income for the "head boat" and crew regardless of the number or kind of fish caught.

A rare solo pound netter, Tom Courtney, 48, clings to the old ways at the southernmost tip of Maryland, near Point Lookout. A St. Mary's College graduate and a Vietnam veteran, he follows in a remarkable fashion the watermen ways of his father and grandfather by continuing to use an ingenious rig called a double-heart pound net.

Paula J. Johnson, a maritime history specialist at the Smithsonian Institution, calls Courtney "by any standard, an extraordinary waterman," not only because of his ways of working the water but for his exceptional daily journals. The Potomac River Fisheries Comission requires a detailed weekly report of the fish caught, but since the early 1970s Courtney has carried that many steps further, keeping track of as many as forty different items, including the sightings of eagles, the nestings of ospreys, and the abundance of jelly fish.

Also a crab potter, the ruggedly handsome bachelor is perpetually ruddy-faced, because his outdoor pace is relentless year-around. When he isn't working on the water, he's busy maintaining his equipment and property on Smith Creek at the dead end of Wynne Road. And if all that isn't enough, he also owns a seafood restaurant and bar (Courtney's) at water's edge.

State marine biologists are continually amazed at his work pace and speak of him in wonder. "I work eight days a week," says Courtney, who, interviewed in his bar, answers questions quickly and in sometimes mumbled sentences, often short on explanation, while chomping down on homemade chocolate chip cookies.

He seems abrupt, but he is usually in too much of a hurry to do something to sit around talking about what he does. A keen observer and recorder of the natural cycle of seafood on the Bay, Courtney blames "too many government regulations" for many of his problems.

"But what pisses me off more than anything is the damn glut of rockfish," he says. "I can't fish because of all the rockfish." He says his nets are full of them and "when they're out of season, I spend far too much time throwing them out and separating them from the elwyes" (an oily, inedible species of menhaden used for crab bait and fishing "chum").

Courtney, who sounds like Jimmy Carter and looks a bit like an unkempt President Clinton, begins in early February pile driving the first of about 350, 35-foot-long pine stakes for his four or five nets. He has to take them all up before the next winter, or the ice could raise and break them. Each stake, sharpened at one end, weighs about 200 pounds (dry). He does require a helper to set them in place and pound them in with a pile driver just offshore in about 18 feet of water. He paints the submerged sections with an anti-fouling paint ($75 a gallon).

The pound nets are intricate rigs with an outer hedging (fence) set up in a straight line several hundred feet long. The fence stops and directs fish into a big heart-shaped enclosure, that, in turn, funnels into a smaller heart-shaped enclosure and then into a rectangular trap called a crib, head, or pound.

Courtney sets up the first of his series of nets just inside the mouth of the Potomac, off Cornfield Point. Others are placed along the Potomac shoreline and in Calvert Bay and Smith Creek, within sight of his restaurant, which serves his fresh seafood catches. He can "fish" (harvest) his pounds several times a day, speeding to and from them at 30 knots in one of his two 24-foot workboats, named "I Corps" and "MACV."

"I fish the same grounds that my grandfather did when he came here in the 1880s from Long Island, where his family were whalers," says Courtney. "I used to fish with my father and grandfather when I was 4 years old. I was the boat bailer."

During the late nineteenth century and into the twentieth century, netting of various forms was the principal method for landing large quantities of fish in the Bay. Commercial fishing in St Mary's County waters was an industry by 1750. The pound net concept was first introduced successfully in Virginia waters in the lower Bay, below the Potomac, in the early 1870s by George Snediker, of Long Island. The idea of fishermen trapping fish and simply dipping them out, carrying them to shore, and selling them caught on.

Courtney's meticulous recordkeeping is for economic reasons, because he has to know what to expect and when to expect it. But he also wishes to understand the Chesapeake's ecosystem, and his written historical record saves far more than the mind can remember. There are more than 200 species of fish native to the waters of the lower Potomac and Courtney has recorded 100 of them. Also recorded are the days he drove poles and "tarred," "coppered," or mended his nets.

Rock Hall waterman Larry Simms, 56, president of the 5,000-member Maryland Watermen's Association, agrees with Courtney that overregulation has caused some of the Bay's problems. "We fish for what is plentiful," he says. "We do it seasonally, so it balances out and the natural cycle kicks in. The rockfish moratorium came five years too late and a new regulation to open the season will probably come five years too late." By February of 1993, watermen were netting rock from the mouth to the head of the Bay, landing from 10,000 to 14,000 pounds a day. "Can you imagine, looking at the entire Bay, what numbers of rockfish must be out there?" he says. "So many that they're eating up everything else they can find to eat."

Simms feels that losing the waterman as a species could be as disastrous as losing a seafood species. "The Chesapeake waterman, whose way of life is working on the water, is an endangered species in Maryland, and if we lose him, we'll lose more than anyone seems to realize. What we'll lose is generations of knowledge, because the waterman knows and care about the fish, crabs, oysters, clams, and eels like no one else."

The commercial waterman "is out on the Bay all year round and he's the first to see any changes or degradation," he adds. "He's the watchdog of the Bay. He's out there when no one else is, and he can see what's happening with his own eyes." But watermen don't, as a rule, keep records like Courtney's. He not only observes what is happening, but faithfully notes it in his detailed journal, kept in a looseleaf notebook labeled "FISH 199-."

Pushing 50, Courtney has at last begun to wonder how long he can continue his demanding pace on and off the water. "I work alone because I can't get the right kind of help," he says. "Maybe I'll scale way back, keep a net or two and some crab pots, and concentrate more on running the restaurant."

Somehow, it's difficult to imagine a pale and wan Courtney with his thick hair combed, trapped inside his climate-controlled restaurant behind large dining room windows that overlook Calvert Bay and the wide, enticing Potomac beyond. And what in the world would he find interesting to put in a notebook labeled "RESTAURANT 1995?"

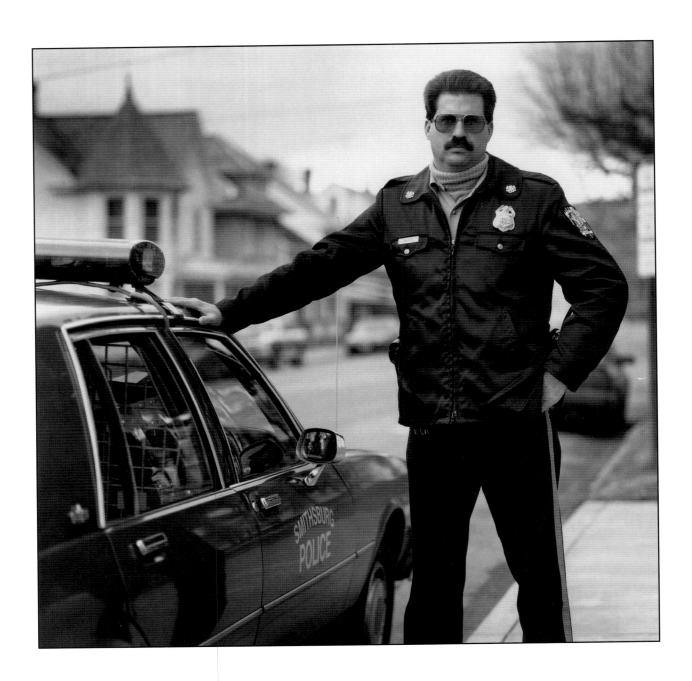

Smithsburg's One-Man Police Force ⌢

In Maryland the lone constable has largely been replaced by police from expanding departments in larger, neighboring jurisdictions, who are able to cover the Main Street beat quickly and in force, if needed. At last report, even television's Mayberry has a two-man department.

As of the winter of 1993, Maryland had three towns with one-person police departments: Chesapeake City in Cecil County, Goldsboro in Caroline County, and Smithsburg in Washington County. Of these, Smithsburg's Charles M. Ender, 31, has the longest tenure, beginning in 1984 when he was elevated from beat patrolman in Hagerstown to chief of police in Smithsburg in one fell swoop.

His office is a small paneled room in Smithsburg's restored town hall, which also houses the mayor, the historical society, and other municipal offices. A sign by the entrance reads, "Police Department," and a reserved parking spot for the chief's 1987 Chevy Capri is right out front.

Chief Ender wears a state trooper–style uniform with a pistol belt and sports a gunfighter moustache, styled hairdo, and manly bearing.

In a corner, a tiny holding space with a cage door waits, the door ajar. This would be known as the town jail, except no one has ever spent the night there, because it contains neither bunk nor toilet facilities. That is not to say, however, that it hasn't been put to use. "We've had some disorderlies awaiting transportation to the lock-up in Hagerstown, but that's about it," says Ender.

Actually, it's usually pretty quiet in Smithsburg (pop. 1,200). There aren't as many stores to rob anymore, and the rewards would probably not amount to much anyway, unless it was a bank hit at a good time. That has happened. On February 2, 1992, one of a series of bank robberies in the county was committed by an armed gang. "We got them twenty-nine days later," says Ender. "I took part in that investigation. It was about the last really exciting thing I handled around here."

Child abuse is on the rise, he says, "and we get a lot of what I call boy and girl disputes, destruction of property, and an occasional breaking-and-entering. I spend a lot of time with paperwork, because this is a very small operation and there's no one else to do it but me."

He patrols a thirty-square-mile area, returning often to the main drag, around

Main and Water streets, where a lot of "No Loitering" signs are posted. "There's not much else for teenagers to do around here other than hang out or squeal wheels to show off for girls," he says. "But that's been going on for a long time, and you're not going to stop it. If too many gather, I just give them a look, flash my lights, and they usually move on."

Things have calmed down considerably since the rowdy Mountain View Tavern was closed and torn down to make room for a bank. There used to be three package liquor stores and five taverns in town. Now, only one saloon remains.

Chief Ender believes his presence keeps things firmly under control. "I can drive around and spot potential troubles," he says. "After a while, you get to know whose cars should be parked where at certain times of the day and night. When a car doesn't belong, you investigate."

Sometimes he can go a week with no calls and won't have even one traffic stop. "That's the way the town likes it, and how I like it, too," he says. "I came here for peace, not action. I got all the action I wanted as a patrolman in Hagerstown. Besides, it would have taken considerably longer to become chief of police anywhere else."

Silversmithing in Baltimore ⁓

In a charming little Lovegrove Alley carriage house, a Baltimore tradition of handworking silver survives at an independent silver smithy operated by the family of Henry Powell Hopkins. Although it still creates and executes original designs for custom work, the firm has evolved into an arts and crafts workshop as well.

Worn wooden work benches are jammed side by side and filled with sterling pieces being restored, rebuilt, refashioned, and created in a space where horses were once stabled. Sawed-off tree stumps stand like butcher blocks, suitable pounding counters for the dozens of specialized, handmade tools of the trade that are stowed in orderly slots throughout the little room.

This is not a retail shop with showcases and a cash register. This is a workshop, and an active one, even though the kind of tools in use here are now collected by museums—as if no one used them anymore.

Henry Hopkins, Jr., 76, son Henry III, 35 (who lives above the shop) and daughter Martha, 33, develop the fine designs that begin the slow path to completion with a rough sketch, which goes through many stages of refinement until they have a finished drawing of the object.

Eventually, handmade wooden "shapes" are turned out on a lathe. The hollowware, for example, is "raised by hand" in one piece with no seams. The base, handle, and spout are handwrought separately. Starting with one sterling disk 12 inches in diameter that resembles a smooth, unfinished plate, the Hopkins family recently crafted an ecclesiastical chalice, paten, and wine flagon that now adorn a church altar in Bel Air.

Since 1950, the senior Hopkins has made ceremonial maces for the American Radiology Society, St. Mary's Seminary, Mount St. Agnes and Washington colleges, the universities of Pennsylvania and Baltimore and Johns Hopkins University, among other institutions. The firm also has a resident engraver, Bill Heymann, 67.

Working with their own handmade shapes the Hopkinses, the last family of silversmiths in downtown Baltimore, delicately and gently hammer the pliable silver disks into shape, a process that can take 200 hours and more.

In another room of the former stable, where a carriage once stood on a now-

inoperable turntable, operations involving soldering, polishing, casting, moldmaking, and kiln burn-outs are conducted.

In dealing with the three-person Hopkins firm, one may at least be assured that all the work originates and is finished in house—unlike some of the work of Maryland's most famous silversmith firms, such as Samuel Kirk, Charles C. Stieff, Heer-Schofield, and A. G. Schultz.

Maryland silver scholar Jennifer F. Goldsborough, chief curator of the Maryland Historical Society, which houses the state's largest collection of sterling, shoots down the popular misconception of "a single colonial silversmith, alone in his small workroom, taking a bag of old coins and creating from start to finish a teapot on which he then struck his initials with the same emotional and artistic investment with which a modern painter signs a portrait." In her book, *Silver in Maryland*, published by the society in 1983, she debunks this "romantic myth fostered by the arts and crafts movement of the late nineteenth century and the reconstructed craft shops of 1930s Williamsburg."

Even on eighteenth-century Maryland silver, she adds, "a particular mark cannot be taken to mean that the man using that mark alone designed, raised, cast, chased, and engraved the piece, but simply that he took the responsibility for guaranteeing to the public the general quality of what might be the work of one or more often anonymous journeymen and apprentices working in his or perhaps even other shops."

By 1830, the majority of Baltimore's silver was being made by Samuel Kirk, whose competition was Andrew E. Warner and, later, Charles G. Stieff. Stieff (founded 1892) and Kirk (founded 1815) merged in 1979, and in 1990 Kirk-Stieff was acquired by Lenox, Inc., which keeps Stieff's Wyman Park manufacturing plant in operation. Today, however, "America's Oldest Silversmiths" turn out mostly die-cast pewter pieces.

One almost vanished art, once practiced by a couple dozen bench craftsmen at Stieff, is called hand-chasing, a technique of "bumping up" sections of a hollow piece of sterling from the inside. Sculpting the raised area into flower and foliage design is called repousse ornamentation.

Repousse, an ancient technique, came into popularity in America in the 1760s and 1770s in Philadelphia and Baltimore. A *nouveau riche* taste for conspicuous consumption prevailed for the next 150 years in Maryland, and the highly decorated look has since become known as Baltimore silver.

Stieff's lone full-time chaser, Nancy Tomlinson, 40, apprenticed under Stieff master chaser Edward Patrick Collins, 69, now retired. Stieff now uses a bumping machine with a laser guide to more accurately bump up the silver. The piece is then filled with pitch to keep the raised areas from sinking during the delicate hand-chasing.

"There is little demand for hand-chased sterling hollowware anymore," says Stieff's resident master silversmith, Keith Franklin, who supervises the annual production of the fully chased Preakness Cup, valued at almost $14,000. "It's far too labor-intensive and expensive for tableware. Nancy is our last chaser, but she's already learning soldering because there's not enough chasing work to keep her busy full time."

The names of Baltimore silversmiths are legend: Lewyn, Boehme, Walraven, Ball, Lynch, Aiken, and Holland, as well as those previously mentioned. Kirk-Stieff, says Goldsborough, is the only important manufacturer of silver and related tableware outside New England.

Maryland silversmiths, Goldsborough assures us, "continue to supply not only their own state's citizens but the entire country with products which keep alive a heritage of good taste, good workmanship, and good living."

The last vestige of this family silversmithing heritage in downtown Baltimore operates not far from where Kirk, Stieff, Schofield, Schultz, and the rest reigned. In keeping with these guarded times, however, the Hopkins family maintains a low profile on Lovegrove Alley. There is no tradesman's sign or house number on the door, but there are iron bars on the windows, a modern burglar alarm system, and a "ring-bell" sign on a locked wooden door.

Once safely past these modern barriers, one enters a world of hand-wrought silver, a vestige of another era, where the almost musical tap-tapping of delicate hammers on soft sterling is heard against an appropriate background of soothing classical music.

Arabbers, Baltimore ⌣

Baltimore's few remaining horse-drawn wagons, driven by fruit and vegetable hucksters known locally as "A-rabbers," still clip-clop through some neighborhoods with harness sleigh bells ringing and the vendors singing. As always, in the summer these charming little painted wagons are filled to capacity in a delicate balancing act, composing a vivid display of edible colors symmetrically stacked and artfully arranged in tiers.

These surviving arabbers (about forty were licensed by the city in 1992) are the only working reminders of a vanished era of horse-and-wagon commerce dating back more than 200 years. They recall a time when deliveries of wood, coal, ice, milk, food, and almost everything else were made by horsecart.

One can still hear the mellifluous, sing-song street hollers of the mostly black arabbers as they fill the sultry summer air, especially in the Hollins Street Market neighborhood, where some of the city's last workhorses, ponies, and wagons are stabled and stored.

These street selling songs are not fully understood by most people, but the generic watermelon cry is immediately recognized by all and it goes something like this:

Wah duh mil yun whoa bee
Wah duh mil yun raid
Raid raid raid
Rine rine rine all raid
To de rine all raid
Whoa bee an' de rine raid too

Translated, the cry announces that the watermelon is "red, red, red; rind, rind, rind; to the rind all red; and the rind is red, too." While one may still hear these cries of street peddlers in the future, they will be coming from modern arabbers, driving light trucks rather than horsecarts.

In the summer of 1992, there were only four active arabber stables in the city, with the oldest, in the Mount Clare neighborhood, dating to the late nineteenth century. This twenty-two-stall stable is owned by white arabber Walter "Buddy"

Kratz, 70, a one-legged man who now arabs from a light truck. Built by Charlie Boyle, the stable was first used to house the mules that pulled city dump carts. Buddy's father, "Buck," bought the stable in 1928, and the son carries on the tradition of renting stalls and hiring out teams and wagons.

The stable, hidden away on Lemmon Street, between Pratt and Lombard streets and tucked in the rear of 112 South Carlton Street, is a two-story brick structure with a hayloft and a yardful of wagons—some large and some almost toylike in size—in various stages of disrepair.

In the courtyard, under a scrubby shade tree, mostly elderly black men and former arabbers hang out and help with various chores associated with running a working stable.

It is a remarkable time capsule, run at a slow pace by Willie "Pistol" Brown, 75, who stables, feeds, grooms, brushes, and looks after the animals. Pistol also tends to leather harnesses festooned with sleigh bells, heart-shaped brass studs, decorative white plastic ringlets, tassels, and red feather plumes. He leads the docile horses and ponies to the waiting wagons and makes certain they are hitched up properly.

There is a timeless, disheveled look to the place, with its fragrant, dark, and murky interior dimly illuminated by bare hanging light bulbs. Nailed to a ceiling floor beam next to a cobwebby exhaust fan is a calendar poster of Jesus Christ, and a crude cardboard sign warning, "ALL PRODUCE WAGONS MUST-IN BY 9:00 PM BY-LAW."

The neighborhood is being renovated and gentrified at a very slow pace, and the future of the stable is inevitable. Kratz realizes its days are numbered. "Every neighborhood had a stable like this, but no more," he says. "You can't open a new stable no more, and you can barely afford to keep the old ones going. It's a dying trade, being replaced by trucks. See them while you can, young man, because they'll soon be gone."

Indeed, one can easily imagine this little dirt courtyard, now surrounded by dilapidated houses and backyards, one day becoming a small pocket park filled with young urban families with baby carriages, not wagons, the stable itself becoming a residential carriage house before the end of the century.

But on any late Saturday morning in the summer one may still observe this dying Baltimore tradition, as a veteran arabber and son of an arabber, Donald Waugh, 58, magically transforms his canopied red and yellow wagon into a moveable, musical market on wooden-spoked wheels.

Waugh prides himself on his artistic arrangement of foodstuffs as he sorts out the market goods in a side alley outside the stable. "We don't be loading the same way every time, because it all depends on what is available at the wholesale market," explains Waugh. Pistol Brown prepares a rented pony named Bum. Renting the rig is Keith Brooks, 32, who, walking alongside holding the bridle, will lead the horse and wagon through the crowded streets, melodically singing his wares from early afternoon to dusk. Balanced at the top of the food pile is a blaring ghetto blaster, along with a hanging scale and a kerosene lantern. Tied to the rear axle is another lantern (a red-glassed tail light) and a galvanized drinking bucket for Bum.

A proud feeling of elitism and camaraderie exists among all arabbers, who are hustlers with street smarts. Says Brooks, "We rarely come home with an empty wagon, and whatever is left over we sell as hog-slopping food." Brooks is joined by a cousin, Gary Hall, whose assignment is to walk ahead of the rig along the sidewalk with a basket of sample goods to show to the customers who appear in doorways when they hear the street cries.

The scholar who has documented this vanishing way of life is Washington folklorist and photographer Roland L. Freeman, himself a one-time arabber and a descendant of arabbers, who has an intimate knowledge of this street clan. In *The Arabbers of Baltimore* he has documented their work with an insider's perspective through memorable photographs. He traces the decline of arabbing to 1966, when Baltimore City placed severe restrictions on any new stable operations, although it "grandfathered" in the few stables that survived urban renewal. At the same time, the city's wholesale produce market, located in the downtown inner harbor area since the 1780s, was moved to the wholesale market at Jessup, 20 miles outside of town.

Arabbers cannot compete with chain food stores, says Freeman, although they still manage to provide a unique doorstep service to those unable to leave their neighborhoods to shop.

They also provide music, in the jingle-jangle of sleigh bells, the handsome baritone cries of the arabbers, and the clippety-clop of gaily festooned ponies pulling colorful, creaking wagons.

The Broom Factory, Baltimore ⁓

A small, two-story, brick and cinderblock building in northeast Baltimore, on a back street corner of North Bradford and an alley named Waldo, appears to be just another abandoned structure in a rundown neighborhood. But on drawing closer, one hears a clanking racket coming from behind the locked doors and sealed windows. There is no sign outside to give a hint of what may be going on inside.

A stable? There is, after all, a sweet smell of straw wafting out through the cracks of one sliding door. After a firm knock the door is opened to reveal a dimly lit scene right out of a Dickens novel.

This working gem of cantankerous clatter from the past is Howard Overman's Broom Factory, dating from the early 1930s, although it looks as if it's been around since the 1830s. Somehow it has survived, although good brooms made in Mexico by cheap labor have swept away all the other broom makers in Maryland. Overman owns the last broom factory in a state that once had dozens, some of them cottage industries operated by the blind to benefit the blind.

Overman, 76, is himself legally blind and must be driven to work, but that has nothing to do with why he makes brooms. The shop was opened by his industrious father during the Depression, after he lost his job. "He was a very hard-working individual and so was my mother, who painted the broom handles." Young Howard became a teenage broom salesman, peddling the merchandise to neighborhood grocery stores. They worked a hard six-day week, fourteen hours a day.

Overman still operates the antique, belt-driven broom-stitching machine that his father taught him to run. It looks like a Rube Goldberg contraption, at once comical and functional, with dozens of parts moving at once. Overman stands at the controls, his foot on a floor pedal. The machine quickly threads five rows of tight, plastic stitching through a broom.

"This machine is at least 60 years old and rarely breaks down," says Overman. A modernized version of the machine is still manufactured by the Baltimore Broom Machine Company, a 100-year-old firm on Sisson Street that continues to supply him with parts when he needs them. Only in Baltimore.

Bare light bulbs dangling overhead dimly illuminate the stablelike interior,

which is heated by a Warm Morning coal stove and a potbellied stove in each of the other two rooms. Working conditions here have changed little in a half-century. The uneven dirt and cement floors are covered with shards of "broom corn"— the long, sweet-smelling straws shipped here in bundles.

"Even well-made brooms like ours do wear out, you know, and thanks for that," says Overman. "People do a lot of sweeping with a broom and every household needs more than a few. We like that aspect of it."

Brooms in various stages of completion are piled and stacked everywhere. Robert Adkins, 39, has been running the wire spool operation for two decades in the front room. In a fragrant, straw-filled back room Tony Cucina, 48, a broom maker here for thirty years, trims the sweeping end with a sharp cutting machine and readies the finished brooms for shipping.

Adkins is the first to arrive, at 6:30 a.m., to fire up the coal stoves. "We start the day all bundled up in the winter and shed our garments as the place warms up," he says. "In the summer, we have fans for air conditioning."

This fast-moving trio can turn out nearly 1,000 brooms a week. Most of them go to janitorial supply houses, hotels, and retail stores. They sell for around $8, although you can buy one at the shop for much less. But Overman discourages retail purchases at the shop, because he is much too busy making brooms to sell them.

"I don't know how much longer this operation will go on," says Overman, whose broom-making father died in 1956. "Brooms are still made in the South and the Midwest, but the competition from Mexico has killed off all the broom makers in Maryland. I guess I'm the last of the Mohicans. There is no member of my family to follow in my footsteps here. I made sure my children had college educations."

Both of Overman's remaining employees arrived as teenagers, "We used to have eight workers squeezed into these cramped quarters," he says. Even with just the three of them, they're still squeezed into cramped quarters.

216

The Last Cupola Caboose, Baltimore ⌣

Finding a caboose in Maryland is easy, even though they have all but vanished from the tail end of freight trains. Just check out a railroad museum or ask a rail fan (there are far more of them than cabooses) for the locations of these outmoded cars that have been converted to shops or getaway vacation cabins or have joined steam locomotives frozen in place in public parks.

Finding a working caboose, however, is something else again, especially a cupola caboose as opposed to the more modern bay window caboose. My hunt for this disappearing breed began at CSX Transportation headquarters in Jacksonville, Florida, and led down through the ranks to CSX's freight yards in Curtis Bay.

"You're looking for a working cupola caboose?" asked Robert J. Comer, Curtis Bay terminal trainmaster. "They're long gone, but we might have one bay window caboose still working. We've replaced cabooses with computerized 'end-of-train,' EOT, devices. Nah, we don't have any more cupola caboo . . ."

Staring out his office window overlooking the freight yards, Comer stopped in mid-sentence: "Wait a minute! I don't believe it! A cupola caboose is going by my window right now. I didn't even know we had one working."

The blue and gray cupola caboose he saw still bears the sleeping cat Chessie System insignia and is the last one working out of Baltimore. An old Western Maryland end-of-train car, it was built in 1936 and looks every bit of it.

It came rolling into the Curtis Bay "Sea Wall" yards one day out of Hanover, Pennsylvania, working the sixty-mile Hanover turn-around route to Baltimore. It was still needed, because the particular freight train to which it was attached makes many stops and back-ups as it moves cars in and out of various industrial plants. But this work pattern will change and probably doom the old steel caboose to the Curtis Bay scrapyard.

"Of course, rail fans know about this particular car," says Baltimore conductor Leon Summers, 51. In his thirty-third year as a railroader and one of CSX's last human end-of-train devices, he is always waving back at people waving at him. "They are always out with their cameras and videocams waiting for us to round a bend or cross a bridge," he says.

Ten years ago there were 12,500 working cabooses in the United States, but the numbers have been drastically reduced, and they are no longer being repaired after major breakdowns.

The disappearing caboose, on the road towards obsolence for years, is a victim of railroad automation and was targeted for total elimination by the mid-1980s after state laws mandating caboose use were repealed. On future routes, conductor Summers, who was assigned to cabooses with a flagman (another position now vanished), will join the engineer and head brakeman in the cab of the locomotive, where the EOT device attached to the end car will be monitored.

"The caboose may look like a cute and charming little cabin on wheels, but I'm here to tell you that living in one was a hobo life," says Summers. "They were ice boxes in winter, ovens in summer, shook your teeth loose with their rough box-car rides, and were absolutely filthy. We called them 'crummies.'"

But after the demise of steam locomotives, some forty-five years ago, cabooses survived as the last traditional link to the romance of the freight train. Dating to the 1850s, they served as rolling observation towers, from which the crews could watch the train ahead and signal to the engineer to stop if something was wrong.

Also known as the doghouse, bird cage, bone breaker, and snake wagon, they were equipped with balconies, porches, and a deck and were the trainmen's living room, dining room, bedroom, kitchen, den, office, workshop, equipment storage room, toilet, and home away from home.

Baltimore's last working cupola caboose is no longer heated with a potbellied coal stove (it was updated to a kerosene space heater) and Summers rarely, if ever, climbs the steel ladders leading to the upper bunks on either side and the cupola's rooftop lookout.

Communicating through a two-way radio with the engineer and brakeman at the front of the train from his perch at the tail end of the train, Summers is not a sentimentalist, although he does realize he has become part of Maryland's railroading history.

As the twenty-five-ton anachronism creeps out of the Curtis Bay Yards toward Westport and beyond, Summers the conductor and human EOT device stands at the brake wheel and waves a farewell with his short-cuffed work gloves.

Hanging on a frame nearby is a twenty-five-pound striped box with an automatic, microelectronic monitor and a red lamp, waiting to replace Western Maryland caboose number 901803, to signal the end of the line for the end of the freight train caboose in Baltimore.